DATE DUE

Modern Critical Interpretations

Thomas Pynchon's
Gravity's Rainbow

Modern Critical Interpretations

These and other titles in preparation

Modern Critical Interpretations

Thomas Pynchon's
Gravity's Rainbow

Edited and with an introduction by
Harold Bloom
Sterling Professor of the Humanities
Yale University

Chelsea House Publishers ◊ *1986*

NEW YORK ◊ NEW HAVEN ◊ PHILADELPHIA

© 1986 by Chelsea House Publishers, a division of Chelsea House
Educational Communications, Inc.

    133 Christopher Street, New York, NY 10014
    345 Whitney Avenue, New Haven, CT 06511
    5014 West Chester Pike, Edgemont, PA 19028

Introduction © 1986 by Harold Bloom

Printed and bound in the United States of America

∞ The paper used in this publication meets the minimum requirements
of the American National Standard for Permanence of Paper for Printed
Library Materials, Z39.48–1984.

Library of Congress Cataloging-in-Publication Data
Thomas Pynchon's Gravity's rainbow.
    (Modern critical interpretations)
    Bibliography: p.
    Includes index.
    Summary: A collection of critical essays on Pynchon's "Gravity's
Rainbow" arranged in chronological order of publication.
    1. Pynchon, Thomas. Gravity's rainbow.   [1. Pynchon, Thomas.
Gravity's rainbow.   2. American literature — History and criticism]
I. Bloom, Harold.   II. Series.
PS3566.Y55G739   1986   813'.54   86–9525
ISBN 1–55546–062–3 (alk. paper)

Contents

Editor's Note

This book gathers together a representative selection of the best criticism yet published upon Thomas Pynchon's encyclopedic novel *Gravity's Rainbow,* arranged in the chronological order of its original publication. I am grateful to Thomas Pepper, Peter Childers, and Susan Laity for their assistance in editing this volume.

The editor's introduction provides a close reading of the story of Byron the Bulb, a crucial vignette in the novel. Richard Poirier begins the chronological sequence of criticism with his strong review of *Gravity's Rainbow,* a review that suggestively compares Pynchon, in his deliberate vulnerability, to both Dreiser and Whitman. In an exegesis of the sadomasochistic episode of Brigadier Pudding and the Mistress of the Night, Paul Fussell illuminates one of the crucial aspects of Pynchon's gospel of sadoanarchism.

The encyclopedic nature of *Gravity's Rainbow* is analyzed by Edward Mendelson in terms of interfaces, modes of living, whether in the book or in the world, that are conditioned by our characteristic labors. Louis Mackey, handling the grand Pynchonian themes of paranoia and preterition (being not of the Elect), declares that the novelist assigns his readers both modes of freedom, the reader-as-paranoid and the reader-as-preterite.

A synoptic reading by Tony Tanner balances the Counterforce's good intentions and its inane performances, rather more darkly than the editor's introduction does. Craig Hansen Werner, noting both Joyce's influence upon *Gravity's Rainbow* and Pynchon's defenses against that influence, sees in Pynchon's agon a moral distrust of all endeavors to compress reality within systems. In a final reading, Gabriele Schwab traces a utopian dimension in the novel, seeing the book as Pynchon's strenuous quest to compel the reader to make sense of an immensely difficult pattern, if only so as to make each reader's paranoia a touch more creative.

Introduction

We all carry about with us our personal catalog of the experiences that matter most — our own versions of what they used to call the Sublime. So far as aesthetic experience in twentieth-century America is concerned, I myself have a short list for the American Sublime: the war that concludes the Marx Brothers' *Duck Soup;* Faulkner's *As I Lay Dying;* Wallace Stevens's "The Auroras of Autumn"; nearly all of Hart Crane; Charlie Parker playing "Parker's Mood" and "I Remember You"; Bud Powell performing "Un Poco Loco"; Nathanael West's *Miss Lonelyhearts;* and most recently, the story of Byron the light bulb in Pynchon's *Gravity's Rainbow.*

I am not suggesting that there is not much more of the Sublime in *Gravity's Rainbow* than the not quite eight pages that make up the story of Byron the Bulb. Pynchon is the greatest master of the negative Sublime at least since Faulkner and West, and if nothing besides Byron the Bulb in *Gravity's Rainbow* seems to me quite as perfect as all of *The Crying of Lot 49,* that may be because no one could hope to write the first authentic post-Holocaust novel and achieve a total vision without fearful cost. Yet the story of Byron the Bulb, for me, touches one of the limits of art, and I want to read it very closely here, so as to suggest what is most vital and least problematic about Pynchon's achievement as a writer, indeed as the crucial American writer of prose fiction at the present time. We are now, in my judgment, in the Age of John Ashbery and of Thomas Pynchon, which is not to suggest any inadequacy in such marvelous works as James Merrill's *The Changing Light at Sandover* or Philip Roth's *Zuckerman Bound* but only to indicate one critic's conviction as to what now constitutes the Spirit of the Age.

For Pynchon, ours is the age of plastics and paranoia, dominated by the System. No one is going to dispute such a conviction; reading the *New York Times* first thing every morning is sufficient to convince one that not even Pynchon's imagination can match journalistic irreality. What is more startling about

Pynchon is that he has found ways of representing the impulse to defy the System, even though both the impulse and its representations always are defeated. In the Zone (which is our cosmos as the Gnostics saw it, the *kenoma* or Great Emptiness) the force of the System, of They (whom the Gnostics called the Archons) is in some sense irresistible, as all overdetermination must be irresistible. Yet there is a Counterforce, hardly distinguished in its efficacy, but it never does (or can) give up. Unfortunately, its hero is the extraordinarily ordinary Tyrone Slothrop, who is a perpetual disaster, and whose ultimate fate, being "scattered" (rather in the biblical sense), is accomplished by Pynchon with dismaying literalness. And yet — Slothrop, who has not inspired much affection even in Pynchon's best critics, remains more hero than antihero, despite the critics, and despite Pynchon himself.

There are more than four hundred named characters in *Gravity's Rainbow*, and perhaps twenty of these have something we might want to call personality, but only Tyrone Slothrop (however negatively) could be judged a self-representation (however involuntary) on the author's part. Slothrop is a Kabbalistic version of Pynchon himself, rather in the way that Scythrop the poet in Thomas Love Peacock's *Nightmare Abbey* is intentionally a loving satire upon Peacock's friend the poet Shelley, but Kabbalistically is a representation of Peacock himself. I am not interested in adding *Nightmare Abbey* to the maddening catalog of "sources" for *Gravity's Rainbow* (though Slothrop's very name probably alludes to Scythrop's, with the image of a giant sloth replacing the acuity of the Shelleyan scythe). What does concern me is the Kabbalistic winding path that is Pynchon's authentic and Gnostic image for the route through the *kelippot* or evil husks that the light must take if it is to survive in the ultimate breaking of the vessels, the Holocaust brought about by the System at its most evil, yet hardly at its most prevalent.

The not unimpressive polemic of Norman Mailer — that Fascism always lurks where plastic dominates — is in Pynchon not a polemic but a total vision. Mailer, for all his legitimate status as Representative Man, lacks invention except in *Ancient Evenings*, and there he cannot discipline his inventiveness. Pynchon surpasses every American writer since Faulkner at invention, which Dr. Samuel Johnson, greatest of Western literary critics, rightly considered to be the essence of poetry or fiction. What can be judged Pynchon's greatest talent is his vast control, a preternatural ability to order so immense an exuberance at invention. Pynchon's supreme aesthetic quality is what Hazlitt called *gusto*, or what Blake intended in his Infernal proverb: "Exuberance is Beauty."

Sadly, that is precisely what the Counterforce lacks: gusto. Slothrop never gives up; always defeated, he goes on, bloody and bowed, but has to yield to entropy, to a dread scattering. Yet he lacks all exuberance; he is the American as conditioned reflex, colorless and hapless.

Nothing holds or could hold *Gravity's Rainbow* together—except Slothrop. When he is finally scattered, the book stops, and the apocalyptic rocket blasts off. Still, Slothrop is more than a Derridean dissemination, if only because he does enable Pynchon to gather together seven hundred and sixty pages. Nor is *Gravity's Rainbow* what is now called "a text." It is a novel, with a beginning, an end, and a monstrous conglomerate of middles. This could not be if the *schlemiel* Slothrop were wholly antipathetic. Instead, he does enlist something crucial in the elitest reader, a something that is scattered when the hero, poor Plasticman or Rocketman, is apocalyptically scattered.

Pynchon, as Richard Poirier has best seen and said, is a weird blend of the esoteric and insanely learned with the popular or the supposedly popular. Or, to follow Pynchon's own lead, he is a Kabbalistic writer, esoteric not only in his theosophical allusiveness (like Yeats) but actually in his deeper patterns (like Malcolm Lowry in *Under the Volcano*). A Kabbalistic novel is something beyond an oxymoron not because the Kabbalah does not tell stories (it does) but because its stories are all exegetical, however wild and mythical. That does give a useful clue for reading Pynchon, who always seems not so much to be telling his bewildering, labyrinthine story as writing a wistful commentary upon it as a story already twice-told, though it hasn't been, and truly can't be told at all.

II

That returns us to Byron the Bulb, whose story can't be told because poor Byron the indomitable really is immortal. He can never burn out, which at least is an annoyance for the whole paranoid System, and at most is an embarassment for them. They cannot compel Byron to submit to the law of entropy, or the death drive, and yet they can deny him any context in which his immortality will at last be anything but a provocation to his own madness. A living reminder that the System can never quite win, poor Byron the Bulb becomes a death-in-life reminder that the System also can never quite lose. Byron, unlike Slothrop, cannot be scattered, but his high consciousness represents the dark fate of the Gnosis in Pynchon's vision. For all its negativity, Gnosticism remains a mode of transcendental belief. Pynchon's is a Gnosis without transcendence. There is a Counterforce, but there is no fathering and mothering abyss to which it can return.

And yet the light bulb is named Byron, and is a source of light and cannot burn out. Why Byron? Well, he could hardly be Goethe the Bulb or Words-worth the Bulb or even Joyce the Bulb. There must be the insouciance of personal myth in his name. Probably he could have been Oscar the Bulb, after the author of *The Importance of Being Earnest* or of that marvelous fairy tale "The Remarkable Rocket." Or perhaps he might have been Groucho the Bulb. But Byron the Bulb is best, and not merely for ironic purposes. Humiliated but immortal, this Byron, too, might proclaim:

> But there is that within me which shall tire
> Torture and Time, and breathe when I expire;
> Something unearthly, which they deem not of,
> Like the remembered tone of a mute lyre.

Byron the Bulb is essentially Childe Harold in the Zone:

> He would not yield dominion of his mind
> To spirits against whom his own rebell'd.

Like Childe Harold, Byron the Bulb is condemned to the fate of all High-Romantic Prometheans:

> there is a fire
> And motion of the soul which will not dwell
> In its own narrow being, but aspire
> Beyond the fitting medium of desire;
> And, but once kindled, quenchless evermore,
> Preys upon high adventure, nor can tire
> Of aught but rest; a fever at the core,
> Fatal to him who bears, to all who ever bore.

There are, alas, no high adventures for Byron the Bulb. We see him first in the Bulb Baby Heaven, maintained by the System or Company as part of its business of fostering demiurgic illusions:

> One way or another, these Bulb folks are in the business of providing
> the appearance of power, power against the night, without the reality.

From the start, Byron is an anomaly, attempting to recruit the other Baby Bulbs in his great crusade against the Company. His is already a voice in the Zone, since he is as old as time.

> Trouble with Byron's he's an old, old soul, trapped inside the glass
> prison of a Baby Bulb.   .

Like the noble Lord Byron plotting to lead the Greeks in their Revolution against the Turks, Byron the Bulb has his High-Romantic vision:

> When M-Day finally does roll around, you can bet Byron's elated. He has passed the time hatching some really insane grandiose plans — he's gonna organize all the Bulbs, see, get him a power base in Berlin, he's already hep to the Strobing Tactic, all you do is develop the knack (Yogic, almost) of shutting off and on at a rate close to the human brain's alpha rhythm, and you can actually trigger an *epileptic fit!* True. Byron has had a vision against the rafters of his ward, of 20 million Bulbs, all over Europe, at a given synchronizing pulse arranged by one of his many agents in the Grid, all these Bulbs beginning to strobe *together,* humans thrashing around the 20 million rooms like fish on the beaches of Perfect Energy — Attention, humans, this has been a warning to you. Next time, a few of us will *explode.* Ha-ha. Yes we'll unleash our *Kamikaze squads!* You've heard of the Kirghiz Light? well that's the ass end of a firefly compared to what we're gonna — oh, you haven't heard of the — oh, well, too bad. Cause a few Bulbs, say a million, a mere 5% of our number, are more than willing to flame out in one grand burst instead of patiently waiting out their design hours. . . . So Byron dreams of his Guerrilla Strike Force, gonna get Herbert Hoover, Stanley Baldwin, all of them, right in the face with one coordinated blast.

The rhetoric of bravado here is tempered and defeated by a rhetoric of desperation. A rude awakening awaits Byron, because the System has in place already its branch, "Phoebus," the international light-bulb cartel, headquartered of course in Switzerland. Phoebus, god of light and of pestilence "determines the operational lives of all the bulbs in the world," and yet does not as yet know that Byron, rebel against the cartel's repression, is immortal. As an immortal, bearer of the Gnostic Spark or *pneuma,* Byron must acquire knowledge, initially the sadness of the knowledge of love:

> One by one, over the months, the other bulbs burn out, and are gone. The first few of these hit Byron hard. He's still a new arrival, still hasn't accepted his immortality. But on through the burning hours he starts to learn about the transience of others: learns that loving them while they're here becomes easier, and also more intense — to love as if each design-hour will be the last. Byron soon enough

becomes a Permanent Old-Timer. Others can recognize his immortality on sight, but it's never discussed except in a general way, when folklore comes flickering in from other parts of the Grid, tales of the Immortals, one in a kabbalist's study in Lyons who's supposed to know magic, another in Norway outside a warehouse facing arctic whiteness with a stoicism more southerly bulbs begin strobing faintly just at the thought of. If other Immortals *are* out there, they remain silent. But it is a silence with much, perhaps, everything, in it.

A silence that may have everything in it is a Gnostic concept but falls away into the silence of impotence, on the part of the other bulbs, when the System eventually sends its agent to unscrew Byron:

At 800 hours—another routine precaution—a Berlin agent is sent out to the opium den to transfer Byron. She is wearing asbestos-lined kid gloves and seven-inch spike heels, no not so she can fit in with the crowd, but so that she can reach that sconce to unscrew Byron. The other bulbs watch, in barely subdued terror. The word goes out along the Grid. At something close to the speed of light, every bulb, Azos looking down the empty black Bakelite streets, Nitralampen and Wotan Gs at night soccer matches, Just-Wolframs, Monowatts and Siriuses, every bulb in Europe knows what's happened. They are silent with impotence, with surrender in the face of struggles they thought were all myth. *We can't help,* this common thought humming through pastures of sleeping sheep, down Autobahns and to the bitter ends of coaling piers in the North, *there's never been anything we could do.* . . . Anyone shows us the meanest hope of transcending and the Committee on Incandescent Anomalies comes in and takes him away. Some do protest, maybe, here and there, but it's only information, glow-modulated, harmless, nothing close to the explosions in the faces of the powerful that Byron once envisioned, back there in his Baby ward, in his innocence.

Romantics are Incandescent Anomalies, a phrase wholly appropriate to John Ashbery's belated self-illuminations also, defeated epiphanies that always ask the question: Was it information? The information that Pynchon gives us has Byron taken to a "control point," where he burns on until the committee on Incandescent Anomalies sends a hit man after him. Like the noble Lord Byron, who was more than half in love with easeful death before he went off to die in Greece, Byron the Bulb is now content to be recycled also, but he is bound upon his own wheel of fire, and so must continue as a now involuntary prophet and hero:

But here something odd happens. Yes, damned odd. The plan is to smash up Byron and send him back right there in the shop to cullet and batch — salvage the tungsten, of course — and let him be reincarnated in the glassblower's next project (a balloon setting out on a journey from the top of a white skyscraper). This wouldn't be too bad a deal for Byron — he knows as well as Phoebus does how many hours he has on him. Here in the shop he's watched enough glass being melted back into the structureless pool from which all glass forms spring and re-spring, and wouldn't mind going through it himself. But he is trapped on the Karmic wheel. The glowing orange batch is a taunt, a cruelty. There's no escape for Byron, he's doomed to an infinite regress of sockets and bulbsnatchers. In zips young Hansel Geschwindig, a Weimar street urchin — twirls Byron out of the ceiling into a careful pocket and Gesssschhhh*win*dig! out the door again. Darkness invades the dreams of the glassblower. Of all the unpleasantries his dreams grab in out of the night air, an extinguished light is the worst. Light, in his dreams, was always hope: the basic, mortal hope. As the contacts break helically away, hope turns to darkness, and the glassblower wakes sharply tonight crying, "Who? *Who?*"

Byron the Bulb's Promethean fire is now a taunt and a cruelty. A mad comedy, "an infinite regress of sockets and bulbsnatchers," will be the poor Bulb's destiny, a repetition-compulsion akin to the entropic flight and scattering of the heroic *schlemiel* Slothrop. The stone-faced search parties of the Phoebus combine move out into the streets of Berlin. But Byron is off upon his unwilling travels: Berlin to Hamburg to Helgoland to Nürnberg, until (after many narrow escapes):

He is scavenged next day (the field now deathempty, columned, pale, streaked with long mudpuddles, morning clouds lengthening behind the gilded swastika and wreath) by a poor Jewish ragpicker, and taken on, on into another 15 years of preservation against chance and against Phoebus. He will be screwed into mother (*Mutter*) after mother, as the female threads of German light-bulb sockets are known, for some reason that escapes everybody.

Can we surmise the reason? The cartel gives up, and decides to declare Byron legally burned out, a declaration that deceives nobody.

Through his years of survival, all these various rescues of Byron happen as if by accident. Whenever he can, he tries to instruct any bulbs nearby in the evil nature of Phoebus, and in the need for solidarity against the cartel. He has come to see how Bulb must move beyond its role as conveyor of light-energy alone. Phoebus has restricted Bulb to this one identity. "But there are other frequencies, above and below the visible band. Bulb can give heat. Bulb can provide energy for plants to grow, illegal plants, inside closets, for example. Bulb can penetrate the sleeping eye, and operate among the dreams of men." Some bulbs listened attentively—others thought of ways to fink to Phoebus. Some of the older anti-Byronists were able to fool with their parameters in systematic ways that would show up on the ebonite meters under the Swiss mountain: there were even a few self-immolations, hoping to draw the hit men down.

This darkness of vain treachery helps to flesh out the reason for Byron's survival. Call it the necessity of myth, or of gossip aging productively into myth. Not that Phoebus loses any part of its profit; rather, it establishes a subtler and more intricate international cartel pattern:

Byron, as he burns on, sees more and more of this pattern. He learns how to make contact with other kinds of electric appliances, in homes, in factories and out in the streets. Each has something to tell him. The pattern gathers in his soul (*Seele*, as the core of the earlier carbon filament was known in Germany), and the grander and clearer it grows, the more desperate Byron gets. Someday he will know everything, and still be as impotent as before. His youthful dreams of organizing all the bulbs in the world seem impossible now—the Grid is wide open, all messages can be overheard, and there are more than enough traitors out on the line. Prophets traditionally don't last long —they are either killed outright, or given an accident serious enough to make them stop and think, and most often they do pull back. But on Byron has been visited an even better fate. He is condemned to go on forever, knowing the truth and powerless to change anything. No longer will he seek to get off the wheel. His anger and frustration will grow without limit, and he will find himself, poor perverse bulb, enjoying it.

This seems to me the saddest paragraph in all of Pynchon; at least, it hurts me the most. In it is Pynchon's despair of his own Gnostic Kabbalah, since Byron the Bulb does achieve the Gnosis, complete knowledge, but purchases that knowledge by impotence, the loss of power. Byron can neither be martyred, nor betray his own prophetic vocation. What remains is madness: limitless rage and frustration, which at last he learns to enjoy.

That ends the story of Byron the Bulb, and ends something in Pynchon also. What is left — whether in *Gravity's Rainbow* or in the immense work-in-progress, a historical novel depicting the coming-on of the American Civil War and reported to have the title *The Mason-Dixon Line* — is the studying of new modalities of post-Apocalyptic silence. Pynchon seems now to be where his precursor Emerson prophesied the American visionary must be:

> There may be two or three or four steps, according to the genius of each, but for every seeing soul there are two absorbing facts, — *I and the Abyss.*

If at best, the *I* is an immortal but hapless light bulb and the *Abyss,* our Gnostic foremother and forefather, is the socket into which that poor *I* of a bulb is screwed, then the two absorbing facts themselves have ceased to absorb.

Rocket Power

Richard Poirier

The fantastically variegated and multistructured $V.$, which made Thomas Pynchon famous in 1963 and the wonder ever since of anyone who has tried to meet or photograph or interview him, is the most masterful first novel in the history of literature, the only one of its decade with the proportions and stylistic resources of a classic. Three years later came *The Crying of Lot 49,* more accessible only because very much shorter than the first, and like some particularly dazzling section left over from it. And now *Gravity's Rainbow.* More ambitious than $V.$, more topical (in that its central mystery is not a cryptogram but a supersonic rocket), and more nuanced, *Gravity's Rainbow* is even less easy to assimilate into those interpretive schematizations of "apocalypse" and "entropy" by which Pynchon's work has, up to now, been rigidified by his admirers.

At thirty-six, Pynchon has established himself as a novelist of major historical importance. More than any other living writer, including Norman Mailer, he has caught the inward movements of our time in outward manifestations of art and technology so that in being historical he must also be marvelously exorbitant. It is probable that he would not like being called "historical." In *Gravity's Rainbow,* even more than in his previous work, history—as Norman O. Brown proposed in *Life Against Death*—is seen as a form of neurosis, a record of the progressive attempt to impose the human will upon the movements of time. Even the very recording of history is such an effort. History-making man is Faustian man. But while this book offers such Faustian types as a rocket genius named

From *Saturday Review of the Arts* 1, no. 3 (3 March 1973). © 1973 by *Saturday Review* Company.

Captain Blicero and a Pavlovian behaviorist named Edward Pointsman, it is evident that they are slaves to the systems they think they master.

For Pynchon the additional comic horror of the Faustianism peculiar to this century is that it can no longer be located in the mad heroics of individuals. It is instead part of the bureaucratic enterprise, of the technological systems that have set history on a course which, like the final descent of the book's rocket, is "irreversible." Any depersonalization of history may therefore be imagined as perverse, with the technological system being turned back upon ourselves in a corporate exercise of masochism like that of one character in the book; she turns her ass to the whip not in surrender but in despair, in order to discover whether she is still human and can cry in pain. The ultimate whip in *Gravity's Rainbow,* the end product of the system, is the supersonic rocket, the German V-2 of the Second World War. It is Moby Dick and the *Pequod* all in one, both the Virgin and the Dynamo of Pynchon's magnificent book.

If in the structure of his books Pynchon duplicates the intricate networking of contemporary technological, political, and cultural systems, then in the style and its rapid transitions he tries to match the dizzying tempos, the accelerated shifts from one mode of experience to another, which characterize contemporary media and movement. As the recurrent metaphors of the book would have it, we are being delivered beyond the human "margin," beyond "gravity," and the natural beauties created by its pressures. Our exhilarations are at the expense of any safe "return," any reentry, except a self-destructive one, into the atmosphere that has made the earth a congenial and precarious "home" for our vulnerable, time-ridden natures.

In Pynchon we "return" to ourselves, come back to the remembered earth of our primal being, reified by the objects to which we have joined our passions, our energies, and our needs. We have become like the young Gottfried, a soldier who allows himself to be placed inside a specially assembled V-2, number 00000, then to be fired beyond the speed of sound, over scenes he thinks he would remember fondly were he able to see them, and down to fiery annihilation.

It is impossible to summarize a book of some 400,000 words in which every item enriches every other and in which the persistent paranoia of all the important characters invests any chance detail with the power of an omen, a clue, to which, momentarily, all other details might adhere. The novel clarifies itself only to create further mysteries, as one such pattern modifies or displaces another. This is a cumulative process with no predictable direction so that any summary is pretty much the product of whatever creative paranoia the book induces in a reader. To complicate matters further, characters are not introduced as they customarily are in fiction, with some brief account of identity and function. Instead, any one of the chapters — which are separated not by numbers but by little squares apparently meant to simulate the sprocket holes in a film — suddenly immerses us in a scene, a mass of persons and furnishings, much as if it were flashed before us on a screen.

In *Gravity's Rainbow* there are some 400 characters all bearing Pynchonesque names (Old Bloody Chiclitz is back, by the way, from *The Crying of Lot 49*), along with a fair number of people who, if you bother, can be found in reference books (e.g., such pioneers in organic chemistry as Kekulé, von Liebig, and Clerk Maxwell). There are scores of submerged references, including one to "The Kenosha Kid." I'd guess this is Orson Welles, born in Kenosha, Wisconsin. A most apt allusion, if one thinks of the hero of *Citizen Kane,* and of how his last word, "Rosebud," is taken as some clue to the lavish assemblage of his wealth and power, when it is instead the name of a little sled, at the end consigned to junk and fire, that he loved as a boy. Any reference or detail in the book can redeem itself this way. But no one of them should ever be regarded as a central clue, and the reader need not fret unduly at what he might miss.

No one, for example, will want to keep track of the hundreds of alphabetical agencies from World War II and the international cartels that are mentioned in the book, nor is anyone expected to. The confusion is the point, and CIA is not what you think it is, but Chemical Instrumentality for the Abnormal. The book is full of disguises, of changes and fusions of identity. The principal character in the main plot is Lt. Tyrone Slothrop, whose ancestry goes back to Puritan stock in colonial New England, but he is sometimes also known as Ian Cuffing, a British correspondent, and sometimes as Der Racketmensch, a title he picks up in Berlin when he sports a cape and helmet looted from a Wagnerian opera company ("*Fickt nicht mit den Racketmensch,*" the poor bastard cries, using a veronica to elude two would-be muggers). He picks up yet another title and another costume in a small German town where, at the behest of some little kids, for whom he will always do anything, he plays the role of Plechazunga, or the Pig Hero, in the yearly pageant to celebrate a tenth-century liberator who appeared in a flash of lightning. He continues to wear his pig costume through a whole series of subsequent adventures.

Aside from the main plot, which deals with a competitive effort to see who can first put together a facsimile of Rocket 00000, there are at least four other major plots, one of which would alone make or enhance the reputation of anyone now writing fiction. There is the story of Lieutenant, later Major, Weissmann, better known by his aforementioned ss code name of Captain Blicero, his love for the Herero tribesman Enzian, both in South-West Africa and in Germany, and his later relationships with Gottfried and with Katje, a double agent who also has an affair with Slothrop. There is the story of Franz Pökler, who was worked on the rocket for Weissmann-Blicero, partly out of fascination but also with the hope thereby of recovering his wife and his daughter Ilse from the concentration camps. There is the story of Tchitcherine, a Soviet intelligence officer, of his exile in central Asia just before the war, his search for his half brother, Enzian, in what Pynchon calls simply "the Zone" after the war, his Koestler-like dialogues with Comrade Ripov, who might have him exterminated, and the subsequent, successful search for him by his German girl, the adoring Geli. And then there is the story of the half brother, Enzian himself, a leader of the *Schwarzkommando* (they are Hereros exiled in Germany for two generations from South-West Africa) and the organizer of their effort to locate all the parts necessary to put together and fire Rocket Number 00001. In all these is a species of travel writing about Berlin before Hitler, London during the Blitz, the Zone after the war, central Asia in the 1930s, German Southwest Africa early in the century—all of it apparently staggeringly authentic not only in researched detail but in tone, in creating the spirit of times and places Pynchon has never seen.

There are also dozens of wondrous ancillary plots featuring characters whose motives and activities are essential to the movement of all the major ones. Probably the most important of these is an elusive Doctor Laszlo Jamf, whose early career as a behaviorist brought him from Darmstadt for a year at Harvard. While there, by agreement between Infant Slothrop's father and I. G. Farben, who will later subsidize Slothrop's education at the same university, Jamf conditioned Infant Tyrone's sexual reflexes. Unfortunately, Jamf's later deconditioning process is ineptly managed so that in London in 1944 Slothrop finds himself getting a hard-on at times and places where the V-2 rocket is to fall.

The phenomenon has not gone unnoticed by Slothrop's superiors, especially Edward Pointsman, in an experimental group called The White Visitation. What mystifies them is that, because V-2 is supersonic, the sound of approach follows rather than precedes the sound of impact. The conceivable stimulus for Slothrop's conditioned response therefore follows the explosion it should warn him about so that, given his repeated proximity to spots where the rocket is to fall, he should be dead. It has to be assumed, therefore, that his conditioning has given him special power of responding not to the rocket sound but to mysterious precursors of its arrival, to some configuration of sights and circumstances. As it turns out, his map of the location of various girls around London perfectly synchronizes with another map kept by the authorities marking V-2 hits. (The reader is free, without any prodding from Pynchon, to play with the joke that perhaps Slothrop's capacity to read signs about the intent of the heavens is part of his Puritan inheritance; he is one of the Elect, one of the Saved.) In any case, Jamf can be said to have programmed the score and bangs for both Slothrop and the rocket, since one of his accomplishments when he later phased himself from behaviorism into organic chemistry was the development of Imipolex G, a plastic essential to the mysterious Rocket 00000.

The central character is the Rocket itself, and all the other characters, for one reason or another, are involved in a quest for it, especially for a secret component, the so-called *Schwarzgerät,* which was wrapped in Imipolex G. Because the multiple search gradually exposes the interlocking relationships among the cultural, economic, and scientific aspects of contemporary life and its historical antecedents, Pynchon can properly refer to it as "the terrible politics of the Grail." Slothrop is compelled because rockets turn him on and because Pointsman contrives to have him observed in his obsession before removing his testicles for analysis. (The designated guinea pig gets away when the wrong man is picked up wearing Slothrop's Pig Hero costume.) Enzian wants to reassemble the Rocket as a final Revelation to his people: the white races who practiced genocide upon them have devised now an instrument of their own annihilation, which is figuratively and, as their firing of the Rocket will show, literally "irreversible." Tchitcherine's pursuit of the rocket is a pretext for finding and destroying Enzian, thus removing the humiliation of having a black half brother. The real powers of the Anglo-American side, whom Pynchon calls "They," indulge Pointsman and Slothrop for the same reason that their Soviet counterparts indulge Tchitcherine — so that They might come into possession of the rocket assembly but, more importantly, so that They might destroy at last the *Schwarzkommando.* "They" want the world to be bleached, as the name Blicero suggests, after Blicker, a folklorish German nickname for Death, for blankness.

What only a few of the various searchers suspect, and what none of Them knows, is the lesson made obvious by the compulsion of the search: the Rocket has taken possession of everyone, and Gottfried is only a physical manifestation of their collective ultimate destiny. Gottfried *is* the *Schwarzgerät,* and Rocket 00000 was assembled in such a way as to make room for his body, covered with an aromatic shroud of Imipolex G. The "secret" is that sex, love, life, death have all been fused into the Rocket's assembly and into its final trajectory.

It can and will be said that such a book as this would have no audience except one prepared by the kind of analytic study of literature that has been in vogue for some thirty years. It's been said already of *V.* and of the works of other related contemporary novelists like William Burroughs, who shares, by the way, Pynchon's marvelous sensitivity to the metaphysical implications of technology, especially film technology, and the way the mind can schizophrenically work like a film projector. But the argument that writers like Pynchon and Burroughs are a by-product of contemporary literary criticism is trivial, since, for one reason, the two books — *Moby-Dick* and *Ulysses* — that come to mind most often as one reads

Gravity's Rainbow indulged in the same kind of complexity, not because criticism had made it fashionable to do so, but because the internal nature of culture made it necessary. And it is further beside the point because *Gravity's Rainbow* marks an advance beyond either book in its treatment of cultural inheritances, an advance that a merely literary education and taste will either distort or find uncongenial.

However outwardly similar, these three works do not conceive of the world in the same way. For historical reasons alone, including a radically changed idea about the structure of human personality, they would have to be vastly different from one another. Where they are alike is in the obligation, assumed without condescension, to shape the world occasionally in compliance with techniques developed outside literature or high culture. All three books take enormous, burdensome responsibility for the forces at work in the world around them, for those "assemblies" of life, like movies, comics, and behavioristic psychology, that go on outside the novel and make of reality a fiction even before a novelist can get to it. That is why all three books are full of renditions of styles and forms other than those derived from literature itself. The rhetoric in *Moby-Dick* often owes as much to the political oratory of Melville's own time as to the works of Shakespeare. *Ulysses* has as much of the newspaper and the music hall as of Homer. Film is everywhere in *Gravity's Rainbow*. So is musical comedy—any given scene might break into a lyric. So are comic books, and although Plastic Man and Sundial are directly mentioned, Superman, Batman, and Captain Marvel, the superheroes of the World War II comics, determine the tone and the conduct of many of the characters.

This kind of thing is now familiar enough, but what distinguishes Pynchon in *Gravity's Rainbow*, especially from such writers as John Barth and Borges, is that he does not, like them, make use of technology or popular culture or literary convention in an essentially parodistic spirit, though he tended to do so in *V*. He is not so literary as to think it odd, an in-joke, that literary techniques are perhaps less powerfully revealing about human nature and history than are scientific ones.

Pynchon, who was a student of engineering at Cornell, knows and respects the imagination embedded in the instrumentalities of science. If he is a scholar of film and super-comics, he is, even more, a scholar of mathematics. There are learned disquisitions on, among other things, organic chemistry and the theory of pauses in classical music, the possibilities of "dodecaphonic democracy" where all the notes in a work get equal hearing, something Pynchon might have gotten from Glenn Gould. Whether or not there is "dodecaphonic democracy" in Beethoven, there is most surely a kind of cultural democracy in Pynchon, and it is different from that in Melville or Joyce, the latter of whom shows a high-cultural nostalgia that is absent from Pynchon. Pynchon is apt to wax nostalgic about lost moments of American adolescence, especially moviegoing, and his idea of character derives more from cinematic media, post-Freudian psychology, and drugs than from other fiction.

Pynchon is willing and able, that is, to work from a range of perspectives infinitely wider, more difficult to manage, more learned than any to be found elsewhere in contemporary literature. His genius resides in his capacity to see, to see feelingly, how these various perspectives, apparently so diverse and chaotic, are begotten of the same technology, the same supportive structures that have foundations in the theology of the seventeenth century and the science of the nineteenth. A good example is his exploration into what are called "frames" in photography, the relation of "frames" to acceleration in moving pictures and in rocketry, and the consequence of this relationship to the human image. About Pökler's work on the rocket, we are told that, in prewar experiments, models of the rocket were dropped by Heinkel airplanes from 20,000 feet and that "the fall was photographed by Askania Cinetheodolite rigs on the ground. In the daily rushes you would watch the frames around 3,000 feet, where the model broke through the speed of sound. There has been this strange connection between the German mind and the rapid flashing of successive stills to counterfeit movement, for at least two centuries — since Leibniz, in the process of inventing calculus, used the same approach to break up the trajectories of cannon balls through the air. And now Pökler was about to be given proof that these techniques had been extended past images on film, to human lives."

This kind of speculative writing abounds in the book, brilliantly bringing together technological and much earlier analytical methods that combine to the eventual distortion of lives. Such passages indicate a dimension of mind and of meditative interest that combines the talents of Henry Adams with the talents of Henry James. One thinks of similar excursions in Mailer, but it is precisely Mailer's limitation that he hasn't shown the courage to admit, as Pynchon continually does, that there are forms of inquiry into the nature of life that are beyond the reach of the Novelist's imagination (Mailer's self-enhancing capitalization), that the Novelist's imagination is often less inclusive or daring than the imagination of mathematics or organic chemistry.

It is not enough to say that Pynchon records the effects of technology on human lives or adapts the methods of technology to the investigation and dramatization of them. Any number of writers have done and are doing that. What he is doing is of far more historical and literary significance. He is locating the kinds of human consciousness that have been implanted *in* the instruments of technology and contemporary methods of analysis; not content with recording the historical effect of these, he is anxious to find our history *in* them. Kekulé's dream, in which he discovered the shape of the benzine ring, the basis of aromatic chemistry, is as beautiful to Pynchon, as humanly revealing, as mythological as is any dream in *Finnegans Wake*. In the case of Pökler and his daughter, Pynchon is showing how the poor man comes to recognize the insidious aptness, for someone of his predilections, of the bait and punishment meted out to him by his superiors. He is allowed to see his long-missing daughter once a year — he cannot even be sure whether it is the same girl one year to the next — in a children's town called Zwölfkinder:

"So it has gone for the six years since. A daughter a year, each one about a year older, each time taking up nearly from scratch. The only continuity has been her name, and Zwölfkinder, and Pökler's love — love something like the persistence of vision, for They have used it to create for him the moving image of a daughter, flashing him only these summertime frames of her, leaving it to him to build the illusion of a single child — what would the time scale matter, a 24th of a second or a year (no more, the engineer thought, than in a wind tunnel, or an oscillograph whose turning drum you could speed or slow at will . . .)?"

She is what Pökler calls his "movie child," the more so since he remembers that on the night of her conception he had been aroused to sex with her mother by a porno film of the 1930s starring one Margherita Erdman, later to be a sometime bedmate of Slothrop. The loved child was in that sense begotten of a film and has since become as if "framed" by film, just as Gottfried is at last "framed" by the Rocket that Pökler helped develop. And both film and Rocket derive from the same analytical and technological legacies.

Everybody in the novel is to some extent similarly "framed," and in the various senses imagined in the wistfully recurrent references to John Dillinger coming out of the Biograph moviehouse, the movie images not yet faded from Dillinger's eyeballs (they are images of Clark Gable going manfully to the chair), Dillinger walking into the ambush prepared for him. At the end of *Gravity's Rainbow* Slothrop, the most "framed" of all, is given a piece of cloth by his buddy, the brawling sailor Bodine, who claims he dipped it in Dillinger's blood that night in Chicago. Dillinger got out of the "frame" only by dying, Gottfried by annihilation, Slothrop finally by some gradual dispersal of self, once the "framed" need to find the Rocket has expended itself. He more or less simply gets lost in the novel, begins to "thin, to scatter," until it's doubtful that he can ever be "found" again in the conventional sense of "positively identified and detained."

The only good way out of the "frame" would have been a saving surrender to peripheral vision. Apparently, it is only there that love is possible, especially love for Pynchon with his extraordinary affection for adolescent girls. As Slothrop sits with Bianca, Margherita's sweet little daughter, herself the offspring of film — conceived while her mother participated in the orgy that would later excite Pökler and lead to the conception of Ilse, the other "movie child" — he senses the timid and frightened desires in her. She wants to escape being "framed." He remembers similar glimpses of possibility when, as a kid, he wheeled around the roads of his hometown in New England, on the lookout for girls:

"Her look now—this deepening arrest—has already broken Slothrop's seeing heart: has broken and broken, that same look swung as he drove by, thrust away into twilights of moths and crumbling colony, of skinny clouded-cylinder gas pumps, of tin Moxie signs gentian and bitter sweet as the taste they were there to hustle on the weathered sides of barns, looked for how many Last Times up in the rear view mirror, all of them too far inside metal and combustion, allowing the days' targets more reality than anything that might come up by surprise, by Murphy's Law, where the salvation could be."

Even while being unpretentiously exact, these images of an American adolescence seem, in their very substantiality, to belong to the images of "framing," which in turn belong to the whole historical vision of the book. The vision confirms itself not by generalization or by abstraction but as a natural emanation from a mind in which ideas are saturated in the color, texture, and minuteness of daily experience. There are of course any number of other, equally reverberating structurings or assemblies, but a good many of them are designedly without this kind of human poignancy. One obvious example is the sign of double integrals, resembling two elongated S's. It is at once a mathematical principle behind the velocity rate of the Rocket, the insignia of the ss, the shape of the tunnels at Nordhausen, the shape of lovers side by side in bed; in physics, the symbol of entropy is S. This kind of patterning has become a tiresome game, and in Pynchon it is, when blatant, usually the object of high spoofing, a symptom of mechanical paranoia.

Readers who get impatient with this book will most likely be too exclusively literary in their responses rather than not literary enough. They'll stare at signs without listening to voices, wonder about characters when they should be laughing at grotesques, and generally miss the experience in a search for the meaning. Above all, they'll be discomfited by a novelist who posits a world in which experience is often most meaningfully assembled in ways considered alternative, often antithetical to literature, like science, or inferior to literature, like film and comic books. It is not possible dogmatically to feel this way about literature and enjoy *Gravity's Rainbow,* or, I would suppose, read the times with much comprehension.

If literature *is* superior to any of these things, then it takes a book as stylistically wide-ranging as *Gravity's Rainbow* to prove it. To know what the book is up to, one must also know the nonliterary genres, so to speak, in which life has been expressing itself. These include not only science and pop culture but the messages sent out by those who usually escape the notice of either, the lost ones, those not "framed," not in the design of things. The signs of their existence are to be found in the waste along the highway, the litter in the trunks of cars, the stuff in the bureau drawer. In his cataloguing of such wastes Pynchon here and in *The Crying of Lot 49* is the most poignant and heartbreaking "realist" since Dreiser.

This is a terribly haunted book. It is written by a man who has totally isolated himself from the literary world of New York or anywhere else. This remoteness is what has freed him from the provincial self-importance about literary modes and manners that is the besetting limitation of writers like Philip Roth — there are some twenty sequences here superior in kind to *The Breast*, accomplished as it is, and at least ten superior to Saul Bellow's *Mr. Sammler's Planet.* Pynchon is almost unbearably vulnerable to every aspect of contemporary experience, open to every form of sight and sound, democratically receptive to the most common and the most recondite signatures of things. "I resist anything better than my own diversity": what Whitman said of himself could be said of Pynchon and of the inexhaustible and elastic powers of synthesis that make his book a kind of assembly of so many other kinds of contemporary assembly, including that of the Rocket.

Pynchon is far too historically intelligent to suggest, however, that the schizophrenic paranoia of his own time is unique to it or that its causes are attributable to that bugaboo Technology. Slothrop can trace his ancestry to a member of Governor Winthrop's crew on the *Arbella,* the flagship of the great Puritan flotilla of 1630, and to a William Slothrop who wrote a nearly heretical book on the relations between the Elect and the Preterite, those who have been passed over, those not elected to salvation. Puritanism is evoked as an early version of the paranoia conditioning us to look for signs of Election and rendering the rest of mankind and its evidences invisible, merely so much waste. The book is therefore a profound (and profoundly funny) historical meditation on the humanity sacrificed to a grotesque delusion — the Faustian illusion of the inequality of lives and the inequality of the nature of signs.

The Ritual of Military Memory

Paul Fussell

Everyone who remembers a war firsthand knows that its images remain in the memory with special vividness. The very enormity of the proceedings, their absurd remove from the usages of the normal world, will guarantee that a structure of irony sufficient for ready narrative recall will attach to them. And the irony need not be Gravesian and extravagant: sometimes a very gentle irony emerging from anomalous contrasts will cause, as Stephen Hewett finds, "certain impressions [to] remain with one — a sunrise when the Huns are quiet, a sunset when they are raising a storm, a night made hideous by some distant cannonades, the nightingales in the warm darkness by a stagnant weedy river, and always the march back from the trenches to reserve-billets in some pretty village full of shady trees." One remembers with special vividness, too, because military training is very largely training in alertness and a special kind of noticing. And one remembers because at the front the well-known mechanisms of the psychology of crisis work to assign major portent to normally trivial things like single poppies or the scars on a rifle-stock or "the smell of rum and blood." When a man imagines that every moment is his next to last, he observes and treasures up sensory details purely for their own sake. "I had a fierce desire to rivet impressions," says Max Plowman, "even of commonplace things like the curve of a roof, the turn of a road, or a mere milestone. What a strange emotion all objects stir when we look upon them wondering whether we do so for the last time in this life." Fear itself works powerfully as an agent of sharp perception and vivid recall. Oliver Lyttelton understands this process in highly mechanical terms:

From *The Great War and Modern Memory.* © 1975 by Oxford University Press, Inc. Originally entitled "Persistence and Memory: The Ritual of Military Memory."

> Fear and its milder brothers, dread and anticipation, first soften the tablets of memory, so that the impressions which they bring are clearly and deeply cut, and when time cools them off the impressions are fixed like the grooves of a gramophone record, and remain with you as long as your faculties. I have been surprised how accurate my memory has proved about times and places where I was frightened.

By contrast, "How faded are the memories of gaiety and pleasure." Subsequent guilt over acts of cowardice or cruelty is another agent of vivid memory: in recalling scenes and moments marking one's own fancied disgrace, one sets the scene with lucid clarity to give it a verisimilitude sufficient for an efficacious self-torment.

Revisiting moments made vivid for these various reasons becomes a moral obligation. Owen registers it in an extreme form, but everyone who has shared his circumstances shares his obsession to some degree. He writes his mother in February 1918: "I confess I *bring on* what few war dreams I now have, entirely by *willingly* considering war of an evening. I do so because I have my duty to perform towards War." Revisiting the battlefields in memory becomes as powerful a ritual obligation as visiting the cemeteries. Of the silent battlefields of Vimy and Souchez, Reginald Farrer says, "They draw and hold me like magnets: I have never had enough." "I still loaf into the past," says Tomlinson, "to the Old Front Line, where now there is only silence and thistles. I like it; it is a phase of my lunacy."

The quality and dimensions of this lunacy of voluntary torment have never been more acutely explored and dramatized than by Thomas Pynchon in *Gravity's Rainbow*. Here for almost the first time the ritual of military memory is freed from all puritan lexical constraint and allowed to take place with a full appropriate obscenity. Memory haunts Pynchon's novel. Its shape is determined by a "memory" of the Second War, specifically the end of it and its immediate aftermath, when it is beginning to modulate into the Third. Just as Harris, Marshall, Robinson, and Burgess have worked up the Great War entirely from documents and written fictions, so Pynchon, who was only eight years old in 1945, has recovered the Second War not from his own memory but from films and from letterpress—especially, one suspects, the memoirs and official histories recalling that interesting British institution of the Second War, the Special Operations Executive (SOE). Like its American counterpart, the Office of Strategic Services, the SOE performed two functions, espionage and sabotage. The unmilitary informality of the SOE's personnel has become proverbial: like an eccentric club it enrolled dons, bankers, lawyers, cinema people, artists, journalists, and pedants. Of its executive personnel the *TLS* observed, "A few could only charitably be described as nutcases." Its research departments especially enjoyed a wide reputation for sophomoric bright ideas and general eccentricity. From the laboratories of its "inventors" issued a stream of cufflink compasses, counterfeit identity documents, plastic explosives, and exploding pencils and thermos bottles and loaves of bread and nuts and bolts and cigarettes. Among booby traps its masterpieces were the exploding firewood logs and coal lumps designed to be introduced into German headquarters fireplaces, as well as the explosive animal droppings (horse, mule, camel, and elephant) for placement on roads traveled by German military traffic. One department did nothing but contrive "sibs" — bizarre and hairraising rumors to be spread over the Continent. It was said that even more outré departments staffed by necromancers, astrologers, and ESP enthusiasts worked at casting spells on the German civil and military hierarchy. Euphemized as "The Firm" or "The Racket" by those who worked for it, the SOE had its main offices at 62–64 Baker Street, and established its departments and training centers in numerous country houses all over Britain.

It is an organization something like the SOE, wildly and comically refracted, to which the American Lieutenant Tyrone Slothrop is assigned in *Gravity's Rainbow.* His initial duties, in September 1944, are to interpret and if possible to predict the dispersal pattern of the V-2 missiles falling on London, a task for which, it is thought, he has a curious physiological talent. This work brings him into contact with numerous colleagues pursuing lunatic researches in aid of Victory: behaviorist psychologists experimenting on (abducted) dogs; parapsychologists persuaded that the application of Schrödinger's *psi* function will win the war; spirit mediums; statistical analysts; clairvoyants; and other modern experts on quantification, technology, and prediction. Their place of work is The White Visitation, an ancient country house and former mental hospital on the southeast coast. The commander of the motley unit at The White Visitation is Brigadier Ernest Pudding, a likable but senile veteran of the Great War called back to preside over this fancy enterprise in the Second War. (In choosing his name Pynchon may be echoing the name of the onetime Director of Operations of the actual SOE, Brigadier Colin Gubbins [born 1896], a badly wounded winner of the Military Cross in the Great War.)

The presence of Brigadier Pudding in the novel proposes the Great War as the ultimate origin of the insane contemporary scene. It is where the irony and the absurdity began. Pudding's "greatest triumph on the battlefield," we are told, "came in 1917, in the gassy, Armageddonite filth of the Ypres salient, where he conquered a bight of no man's land some 40 yards at its deepest, with a wastage of only 70% of his unit." After this satire of circumstance he remained in the army until he retired in the thirties to the Devon countryside, where "it occurred to him to focus his hobby on the European balance of power, because of whose long pathology he had once labored, deeply, all hope of waking lost, in the nightmare of Flanders." In his retirement he pursued the hopeless hobby of writing a massive "book" titled *Things That Can Happen in European Politics.* But events defeated him and his resolution dissolved: "'Never make it,' he found himself muttering at the beginning of each day's work—'it's changing out from under me. Oh, dodgy—very dodgy.'" At the beginning of the Second War he volunteered and was further disappointed:

> Had he known at the time it would mean "The White Visitation"
> . . . not that he'd expected a combat assignment you know, but
> wasn't there something mentioned about intelligence work? Instead
> he found a disused hospital for the mad, a few token lunatics, an
> enormous pack of stolen dogs, cliques of spiritualists, vaudeville en-
> tertainers, wireless technicians, Couéists, Ouspenskians, Skin-
> nerites, lobotomy enthusiasts, Dale Carnegie zealots.

His present situation is especially disappointing because the quality of the person-nel seems to have fallen off between wars. The nutty dog experimenter at The White Visitation, Ned Pointsman, happens to be the son of an able medical of-ficer Pudding knew at Ypres. Ned is "not as tall as his father, certainly not as wholesome looking. Father was M.O. in Thunder Prodd's regiment, caught a bit of shrapnel in the thigh at Polygon Wood, lay silent for seven hours before they"—but the scene clouds over in Pudding's memory and begins to fade: "without a word before, in that mud, that terrible smell, in, yes Polygon Wood . . . or was that—who *was* the ginger-haired chap who slept with his hat on? ahhh, come back. Now Polygon Wood . . . but it's fluttering away." No use: Pudding is losing the image he has been soliciting, and only detached, incoherent details remain: "Fallen trees, dead, smooth gray, swirling-gräinoftreelikefrozen-smoke . . . ginger . . . thunder . . . no use, no bleeding use, it's gone, another gone, another, oh dear."

Sometimes Pudding's memories surface publicly during his prolonged and rambling weekly briefings of the staff, occasions designated by Pynchon as "a bit of ritual with the doddering Brigadier." Mingled with "a most amazing volley of senile observations, office paranoia, gossip about the war," as well as with such detritus as "recipes for preparing beets a hundred tasty ways," are detached, inco-herent "reminiscences of Flanders," little sensual spots of time and images en-graved on the failing memory:

> the coal boxes in the sky coming straight down on you with a roar
> . . . the drumfire so milky and luminous on his birthday night
> . . . the wet surfaces in the shell craters for miles giving back one

bleak autumn sky . . . what Haig, in the richness of his wit, once said at mess about Lieutenant Sassoon's refusal to fight . . . roadsides of poor rotting horses just before apricot sunrise . . . the twelve spokes of a standard artillery piece—a mud clock, a mud zodiac, clogged and crusted as it stood in the sun in its many shades of brown.

Brown triggers in Pudding a little lyric on human excrement as the dominant material of Passchendaele: "The mud of Flanders gathered into the curd-crumped, mildly jellied textures of human shit, piled, duck-boarded, trenches and shell-pocked leagues of shit in all directions, not even the poor blackened stump of a tree."

Such discrete images take on coherence and something like narrative relationships only during Pudding's secret fortnightly "rituals," his surreal nocturnal visits to the "Mistress of the Night," played by Katje Borgesius, a Dutch girl who has somehow become attached to this mock-SOE. The passage in which Pynchon presents one of these ritual visits is one of the most shocking in the novel: it assumes the style of classic English pornographic fiction of the grossly masochistic type, the only style, Pynchon implies, adequate to memories of the Great War, with its "filth" and "terrible smell." The language and the details may turn our stomachs, but, Pynchon suggests, they are only the remotest correlatives of the actuality. Compared with the actual sights and smells of the front, the word *shit* is practically genteel.

It is not easy to specify exactly the "allegorical" meaning of this "Mistress of the Night" to whom the aging brigadier repairs so regularly and punctually: she is at once Death, Fear, Ruined Youth, and the memory of all these. She is what one must revisit ritually for the sake of the perverse pleasant pain she administers. She is like the Muse of Pudding's war memory. She waits to receive him in a setting combining bawdy house with theater, and indeed the scene of Pudding's visit constitutes the climax of the tradition that the Great War makes a sort of sense if seen as a mode of theater.

It is a cold night. Pudding slips out of his quarters "by a route only he knows," quietly singing, to keep his courage up, the soldiers' song he recalls from the Great War:

> Wash me in the water
> That you wash your dirty daughter,
> And I shall be whiter than the whitewash on the wall.

He tiptoes along the sleeping hallways and through a half-dozen rooms, the passage of which, like the traditional approach to the Grail Chapel, constitutes a "ritual": each contains "a test he must pass." In the third room, for example, "a file drawer is left ajar, a stack of case histories partly visible, and an open copy of Krafft-Ebing." The fourth room contains a skull. The fifth, a Malacca cane, which apparently reminds him of the one he carried in 1917 and sets him thinking: "I've been in more wars for England than I can remember . . . haven't I paid enough? Risked it all for them, time after time . . . Why must they torment an old man?" In the sixth and last room the memory of the war becomes more vivid:

> In the sixth chamber, hanging from the overhead, is a tattered tommy up on White Sheet Ridge, field uniform burned in Maxim holes black-rimmed . . . , his own left eye shot away, the corpse beginning to stink . . . no . . . no! an overcoat, someone's old coat that's all, left on a hook in the wall . . . but couldn't he *smell* it? Now mustard gas comes washing in, into his brain with a fatal buzz as dreams will when we don't want them, or when we are suffocating. A machine-gun on the German side sings *dum diddy da da,* an English weapon answers *dum dum,* and the night tightens coiling around his body, just before H-hour.

It is H-hour now, for he has arrived at the seventh room, where the Mistress of the Night waits for him. He knocks, the door unlocks "electrically," and he enters a room lighted only by a "scented candle." Katje Borgesius sits in a throne-like chair, wearing nothing but the black cape and tall black boots of the traditional female "disciplinarian" in British pornography. She is made up to resemble "photographs of the reigning beauties of thirty and forty years ago," and the only jewelry she wears is "a single ring with an artificial ruby not cut to facets" but resembling a convex bloody wound. She extends it, and Pudding kneels to kiss it before undressing.

> She watches him undress, medals faintly jingling, starch shirt rattling. She wants a cigarette desperately, but her instructions are not to smoke. She tries to keep her hands still. "What are you thinking, Pudding?"
> "Of the night we first met." The mud stank. The Archies were chugging in the darkness. His men, his poor sheep, had taken gas that morning. He was alone. Through the periscope, underneath a star shell that hung in the sky, he saw her . . . and though he was hidden, she saw Pudding. Her face was pale, she was dressed all in black, she stood in No-man's Land, the machine guns raked their patterns all around her, but she needed no protection. "They knew you, Mistress. They were your own."

"And so were you."

"You called to me, you said, 'I shall never leave you. You belong to me. We shall be together, again and again, though it may be years between. And you will always be at my service.'"

Pudding now undergoes his ritual of humiliation. He creeps forward to kiss her boots. He excites her by reminding her of an incident in the Spanish Civil War when a unit of Franco's soldiers was slaughtered. She is pleased to remember. "I took their brown Spanish bodies to mine," she says. "They were the color of the dust, and the twilight, and of meats roasted to a perfect texture . . . most of them were so very young. A summer day, a day of love: one of the most poignant I ever knew." "Thank you," she says to Pudding. "You shall have your pain tonight." And she gives him a dozen blows with the cane, six across the buttocks, six across the nipples. "His need for pain" is gratified; he feels momentarily rescued from the phony paper war he's now engaged in, reinstalled in his familiar original world of "vertigo, nausea, and pain." The whipping over, she obliges him to drink her urine. And then the climax of the ritual: he eats her excrement. It is an act reminiscent of their first encounter at Passchendaele: "The stink of shit floods his nose, gathering him, surrounding him. It is the smell of Passchendaele, of the Salient. Mixed with the mud, and the putrefaction of corpses, it was the sovereign smell of their first meeting, and her emblem." As he eats, "spasms in his throat continue. The pain is terrible." But he enjoys it. Finally she commands him to masturbate before her. He does so and departs regretfully, realizing anew, when he reaches his own room again, that "his real home is with the Mistress of the Night."

It is a fantastic scene, disgusting, ennobling, and touching, all at once. And amazingly rich in the way it manages to fuse literal with figurative. The woman is both Katje and the Mistress of the Night, credible for the moment in either identity; she is both a literal filthy slut in 1945 and the incarnation of the spirit of military memory in all times and places. As allegory the action succeeds brilliantly, while its literal level is consistent and within the conventions, credible: Pudding, we are told later, died in June 1945, "of a massive *E. coli* infection" brought about by these ritual coprophagic sessions. And yet what he was "tasting" and "devouring" all the time was his memories of the Great War.

Gravity's Encyclopedia

Edward Mendelson

In both its range and, one may predict, its cultural position, *Gravity's Rainbow* recalls only a few books in the Western tradition. To refer to it as a novel is convenient, but to read it as a novel—as a narrative of individuals and their social and psychological relations—is to misconstrue it. Although the genre that now includes *Gravity's Rainbow* is demonstrably the most important single genre in Western literature of the Renaissance and after, it has never previously been identified. *Gravity's Rainbow* is an *encyclopedic narrative,* and its companions in this most exclusive of literary categories are Dante's *Commedia,* Rabelais's five books of Gargantua and Pantagruel, Cervantes's *Don Quixote,* Goethe's *Faust,* Melville's *Moby-Dick,* and Joyce's *Ulysses.*

Each major Western national culture, as it becomes fully conscious of itself as a unity, produces an encyclopedic author, but not all encyclopedists produce a single encyclopedic narrative. In England the encyclopedic role is divided among the tales of Chaucer and the plays of Shakespeare. The only unified encyclopedic narratives written in England thus arrive too late to fulfill a central cultural role, and are self-consciously aware of the limitations of their belatedness. These encyclopedic latecomers include most notably the mock-encyclopedia *Tristram Shandy* which, like the "Tristra-paedia" it contains, collapses under the weight of data too numerous and disparate for its organizing mechanisms to bear; and the satiric imaginary encyclopedia *Gulliver's Travels,* which fulfills all the formal requirements of an encyclopedia but, through its displacement from Britain into imagined colonies, fails to inhabit the historical and cultural position already securely

From *Mindful Pleasures: Essays on Thomas Pynchon.* © 1976 by George Levine and David Leverenz. Little, Brown & Co., 1976.

occupied by Shakespeare. *Ulysses* resolves the difficulties of an encyclopedia of a belated and marginal Irish culture by acknowledging the political marginality of its protagonist, while asserting the literary centrality and density of the book's relation to the larger culture of Europe.

This is not the occasion for a general theory of encyclopedic narrative, which I hope to supply elsewhere, but it may be useful to construct a model that will serve for the moment. Encyclopedic narratives attempt to render the full range of knowledge and beliefs of a national culture, while identifying the ideological perspectives from which that culture shapes and interprets its knowledge. Because they are the products of an epoch in which the world's knowledge is larger than any one person can encompass, they necessarily make extensive use of synecdoche. No encyclopedic narrative can contain all of physical science, so examples from one or two sciences serve to represent the whole scientific sector of knowledge. One of many points of distinction between epic and encyclopedia is the epic writer's unconcern with fields of knowledge outside his experience. In the ancient epic, no such fields exist, or none of any importance; while in the modern epic, which is generally interiorized or miniature like *The Prelude,* the only knowledge that matters is the knowledge through which a mind creates itself.

Encyclopedic narrative evolves out of epic, and often uses epic structure as its organizing skeleton (Dante, Cervantes, Joyce), but the subjects of epic become increasingly vestigial to the encyclopedic form. Joyce wrote that *Ulysses* was "a sort of encyclopedia," and *Ulysses* probably shows the last extensive use of epic patterns in Western encyclopedic writing. Epics treat of the immediate culture in which they are written only allusively and analogically: epic action is set in a legendary past, and although that action may comment forcefully on the situation of the writer's "present," as does the *Aeneid,* the action takes few of its particulars from the facts of ordinary "present" experience. Encyclopedic narratives are set *near* the immediate present but not in it. The main action of most of them occurs about twenty years before the time of writing, allowing the book to maintain mimetic (or, more precisely, satiric) relation to the world of its readers, while permitting it also to include prophecies that are accurate, having been fulfilled between the time of the action and the time of writing. These "accurate" prophecies then claim implicitly to confer authority on other prophecies in the book which have not yet been fulfilled. Thus Dante begins writing around 1307 about events of 1300, and can easily make his characters prophesy the death of Pope Boniface VIII in 1303. Cervantes lets Don Quixote prophesy the writing of his own history, and Joyce prophesies the authorship of Stephen Dedalus. Pynchon sets the action of his book at the moment which he proposes as the originating instant of contemporary history, a gestative nine months at the end of the

Second World War. Encyclopedic narrative thus achieves the double function of prophecy and satire: it predicts events that are, in reference to the book's action, in the unpredictable future, yet the action is sufficiently close to the moment of publication to allow the book to describe and encompass the familiar details of its readers' lives.

The prophetic quality of encyclopedic narrative—its openness in time—is echoed by its peculiar indeterminacy of form. Generic analysis of encyclopedic narrative yields far more limited results than may be gained from most other varieties of narrative. An encyclopedic narrative is, among other things, an encyclopedia of narrative, incorporating, but never limited to, the conventions of heroic epic, quest romance, symbolist poem, bourgeois novel, lyric interlude, drama, eclogue, and catalogue.

Encyclopedic narrative identifies itself not by special plot or structure but by encompassing a special set of qualities. Almost all encyclopedic narratives share a range of characteristics peculiar to themselves, and these characteristics may, in summary form, be listed briefly. (Near-encyclopedias—*War and Peace, Middlemarch, Bouvard et Pécuchet, U.S.A., One Hundred Years of Solitude,* the work of Balzac and Quevedo—are excluded from the central genre not only by their lack of many or most of these characteristics but also by their failure to occupy a special cultural position.)

All encyclopedic narratives include a full account of at least one technology or science. That is, they correlate the opposed worlds of aesthetic freedom (which is reflected in art) and natural necessity (which is reflected in science) far more elaborately than most other literary works. A complete medieval astronomy may be constructed out of the *Commedia.* Don Quixote explores the pharmacopeia and is an adept at the "science of arms." *Faust* expounds opposing geological theories, and anticipates evolutionary biology. *Moby-Dick* is an encyclopedia of cetology. A detailed summary of embryology is embedded in "The Oxen of the Sun" chapter of *Ulysses,* as is a theory of positivism in "Ithaca." *Gravity's Rainbow* is expert in ballistics, chemistry, and mathematics. An encyclopedic narrative normally also includes an account of an art outside the realm of written fiction: the carved bas-reliefs in the *Purgatorio,* the puppetry of *Don Quixote,* the Greek tragedy in *Faust,* whale-painting in *Moby-Dick,* the musical echoes in *Ulysses's* "Sirens," film and opera in *Gravity's Rainbow.*

Each encyclopedic narrative is an encyclopedia of literary styles, ranging from the most primitive and anonymous levels (all encyclopedias include compendia of proverb-lore, as *Gravity's Rainbow* lists the Proverbs for Paranoids) to the most esoteric of high styles. All encyclopedias metastasize the monstrousness of their own scale by including giants or gigantism: the giants who guard the pit of Hell in Dante, the eponymous heroes in Rabelais, the windmills which Don

Quixote takes for giants, the mighty men whom Faust sends into battle, Moby Dick, the stylistic gigantism of Joyce's "Cyclops," the titans under the earth in *Gravity's Rainbow,* and the angel over Lübeck whose eyes went "towering for miles."

Because encyclopedic narratives appear near the beginning of a culture's or a nation's sense of its own separate existence, and because Melville has already fulfilled the encyclopedic role in North America, Pynchon's international scope implies the existence of a new international culture, created by the technologies of instant communication and the economy of world markets. Pynchon implies that the contemporary era has developed the first common international culture since medieval Latin Europe separated into the national cultures of the Renaissance. The distinguishing character of Pynchon's new internationalism is its substitution of data for goods: "Is it any wonder the world's gone insane," someone asks in *Gravity's Rainbow,* "with information come to be the only real medium of exchange?" Elsewhere, another character explains that the immediate postwar situation is "like the very earliest days of the mercantile system. We're back to that again." The postwar proliferation of new systems and structures is made possible by the elimination of older systems that can no longer function, the collapse of social structures that have grown obsolete: "this War . . . just for the moment has wiped out the proliferation of little states that's prevailed in Germany for a thousand years. Wiped it clean. *Opened it*" (Pynchon's italics).

Pynchon's implied historical claims are enormous, and in any sober reader, should inspire a healthy skepticism. But the book's ambition is essential to its design. No one could suppose that encyclopedic narratives are attractive or comfortable books. Like the giants whose histories they include, all encyclopedias are monstrous (as they are *monstra* in the oldest Latin sense — omens of dire change). None of their narratives culminates in a completed relation of sexual love. Dante's flesh cannot merge with Beatrice's soul; Panurge never gets around to marrying; Dulcinea either does not exist at all, or — if you happen to be reading a different part of the book — she does exist, but Don Quixote has never seen her; Faust loses Margarete a third of the way through the book, then marries and loses the bodiless Helen; Ahab's wife waits on shore for widowhood; Bloom and Molly do not resume the sexual relations they ended a decade ago; and, while Mexico loses Jessica, Slothrop, for all his sexual exuberance, disintegrates lovelessly. The encyclopedic impulse is both analytic and synthetic: in its analytic and archetypally masculine mode, it separates a culture into its disparate elements, while its synthetic, archetypally feminine mode merges them in the common texture of a single book: but it is a law of encyclopedic form that the synthetic mode cannot be localized in a single sexual relationship. Compared with other works by the same authors, encyclopedias find it exceptionally difficult to integrate their women characters into the narrative at any level more quotidian or humane than the levels of archetype and myth.

Encyclopedic narrative strains outwards from the brief moments of personal love towards the wider expanses of national and mythical history, and towards the history of its own medium. All encyclopedias are polyglot books, and all provide a history of language. Dante identifies the dialects of Italy and France and the degenerate language of Nimrod, and in Canto XXVI of the *Paradiso* Adam offers a religious history of language. Panurge begs bread from Pantagruel in thirteen languages (three of them invented for the occasion) before getting around to French. Don Quixote is expert in etymology, especially the effect of Arabic on Castilian. Faust educates Helen out of Greek hexameters into the rhymed stanzas of romance languages. Melville opens his book with a full range of etymologies. Joyce puns in at least seven languages. Pynchon uses French, German, Italian, Spanish, Middle Dutch, Latin, Japanese, Kirghiz, Herero, various English and American dialects—all with their concentrated emblem in the German-Latin macaronic that Roger Mexico and Jessica Swanlake hear in an English church at Christmas. Pynchon also asserts the inclusiveness of his vision through his development and use of three "national" styles: a dignified and elegiac manner employed for British characters and settings, a slangy American dialect that syncopates around Tyrone Slothrop and pretends to be a stream-of-mutterings, and a heightened solemn manner used for German scenes, one which I suspect is meant to recall the prose style of Rilke. (It is noteworthy that the only conventionally modernist sections of the book are the Slothrop sequences, with their private point of view and stream of consciousness. Slothrop's disintegration, Pynchon implies, summarizes the historical fate of literary modernism.)

The difference between the two twentieth-century encyclopedias in English, Joyce's and Pynchon's, appears in an especially emphatic manner in their opposing accounts of language. The *knowledge* of language in Pynchon and Joyce is entirely comparable, but their *histories* of language arise from drastically incompatible visions of both language and the larger world. "The Oxen of the Sun" chapter of *Ulysses* offers a linguistic history on an organic model derived from embryology. Joyce's history is primarily a history of style, and of the effects of style on social conventions. Like an embryo metamorphosing progressively from silent zygote to squalling infant, the styles of Joyce's chapter metamorphose historically from Old English to a drunken garble that staggers through the language of the present. The historical sequence is interrupted only by brief delays and anticipations based on corresponding anomalies in the development of the embryo. Pynchon's corresponding historical linguistics occupies the episode in *Gravity's Rainbow* that follows Tchitcherine to the Kirghiz, and is a history not of style but of the political *use* of language. It is also an exposition of the ways in which language is altered by political decisions, and of the modes in which language affects the world of life and death that lies ultimately outside language.

Read as if it were one element among the conventional structures of a novel, the Kirghiz episode seems disproportionate and anomalous. Its apparent goal, Tchitcherine's vision of the Kirghiz Light, does have analogical relations with other charismatic goals in the book; and the prehistoric city that lies below Tchitcherine "in mineral sleep" as he watches the Kirghiz Light gives local habitation to the strata and processes described by the spirit of Walter Rathenau in an earlier chapter. Tchitcherine's vision almost but (the narrator emphasizes) not quite induces in Tchitcherine himself the emptying and rebirth that takes place on a political level in the book's vision of a disordered Europe. But all the rest of the sequence, concerned as it is with the motives and consequences of the Soviet introduction of a Latin alphabet into illiterate Kazakhstan — what can that have to do with the rest of the book?

Yet once the encyclopedic nature of the book is recognized, the Kirghiz interlude moves from its apparent place at the book's periphery to its ideological and thematic center. Virtually every event in *Gravity's Rainbow* is involved in a political process: specifically, the transformation of charismatic energy into the controlled and rationalized routine of a bureaucracy. These terms are of course borrowed from Max Weber, to whom Pynchon twice attributes the phrase "the routinization of charisma." The history of language in *Gravity's Rainbow* illustrates one version of this process of political organization. For the Kirghiz people, before the arrival of Tchitcherine and his bureaucracy, language "was purely speech, gesture, touch . . . not even an Arabic script to replace." With the introduction of the New Turkic Alphabet, or NTA, whole systems of committees, subcommittees, various divisions of labor and authority now organize and reticulate themselves over the buried strata of the local folk culture. Unlike the language of Joyce's "Oxen of the Sun," the NTA does not develop according to an organic model but is shaped deliberately by the forces of government, forces which are themselves ultimately directed and initiated by the cartels which organize the book's secular world.

The processes that shape the NTA, and with it the Kirghiz language, are enactments, at a relatively modest scale, of world-processes that function throughout the book. But the events of the book cannot be blamed entirely on the political intentions of cartels and governments: the processes that shape events in *Gravity's Rainbow* operate continuously on all levels of the book's reality, including the mythic levels of titans, the bodiless world of the dead, and the submicroscopic level of chemical structure, all of which even the powerful cartels can neither recognize nor control. One of the NTA functionaries, Igor Blobadjian, has a vision in which he is reduced to the size of molecules, and discovers that the political processes in which he participates at the level of the world "above" have their molecular counterparts in the chemical politics of the world "below."

The NTA is shaped by processes that are not merely linguistic, and its effects are felt outside of language. The availability of a written language permits more than the simple act of writing: it makes possible new events not limited to the realm of signs. Pynchon's parenthetical joke gets to the heart of the matter:

> On sidewalks and walls the very first printed slogans start to show up, the first Central Asian . . . kill-the-police-commissioner signs (and somebody does! this alphabet is really something!) and so the magic that the shamans, out in the wind, have always known, begins to operate now in a political way.

The shamans worked curses and blessings through incantations or spells, but now language formulated into writing operates "in a political way." The consequences of this realization have a tragic force. All the book's efforts at truth-telling, all its thrusts at the increase of freedom through the revelation of necessity, are *infected* by the inevitable fact that the book itself must use a language that is, unavoidably, a system shaped by the very powers and orders that it hopes to reveal. Language can never be liberated from lies. One cannot speak outside of language, and one cannot directly speak the truth within it—this not only in the reflexive sense proclaimed by recent critical theory but in a political sense as well. To separate oneself from language, in an attempt to be free from its imposed order, is to enter a world of chaos and vacancy. This tragic realization is at the ideological center as well as on the stylistic surface of the book. *Gravity's Rainbow* does not propose—with the romantic fervor appropriate to such proposals—that you escape the systems of pain and control that occupy and shape the world: the book insists that it is impossible to escape those systems yet retain any decency, memory, or even life—just as it is impossible to escape from language yet communicate. If the connectedness of the world has its metonym in paranoia— "nothing less than the onset, the leading edge, of the discovery that *everything is connected,* everything in the Creation"—then Slothrop's detachment from the world's order and the order of language (he is in the end unable to speak or even to hear) may be called "anti-paranoia, where nothing is connected to anything, a condition not many of us can bear for long."

The NTA episode proposes the linguistic basis for *Gravity's Rainbow,* but it also fortuitously provides us with our first extended glance into Pynchon's workshop. Although the organizing historical intelligence behind each of Pynchon's books may be identified with little difficulty—Henry Adams is named in *V.,* as Weber is named in *Gravity's Rainbow,* and I have presented elsewhere the evidence for Mircea Eliade's shaping presence behind *The Crying of Lot 49*—no one has yet identified a source for any of the *local* clusters of data in Pynchon's work. The NTA episode, if it is in fact as typical of the rest of the book as it appears to be, demonstrates how little of Pynchon's world is built from nothing. In fact, virtually all the historical and linguistic details in the episode derive directly from an article by Thomas G. Winner, "Problems of Alphabetic Reform among the Turkic Peoples of Soviet Central Asia, 1920–1941," in the *Slavonic and East European Reviews* 31 (1952), 133–47. And the Kirghiz folklore, the ajtys, the aqyn, and all the Kirghiz vocabulary of the episode, derive from Professor Winner's book, *The Oral Art and Literature of the Kazakhs of Russian Central Asia* (Durham, 1958). As far as I can determine, however, the Kirghiz Light is Pynchon's own invention.

The scale of the source and the fiction are of course entirely different: Pynchon selects from, and elaborates on, some of the smallest of Professor Winner's details. Pynchon invents a bureaucratic dispute over the spelling of "stenography," a word required in the Kirghiz language only as a consequence of the politically motivated introduction of an alphabet. You don't need a word for stenography if you can't write. The dispute—"a crisis over which kind of g to use," whether a roman g or an ad hoc letter resembling a reversed cyrillic g— exfoliates from a footnote in which Professor Winner lists loan-words in Kirghiz, of which the word for stenography is the only one using the unusual letter. By the end of the episode the whole matter has become embedded in the texture of the narrative: Tchitcherine takes down the Aqyn's song of the Kirghiz Light "in stenography."

One almost hesitates to report a discovery of this kind. Charismatic books tend, like other loci of charisma, to develop a routinized critical bureaucracy around them. Who, witnessing the enormous multinational operations of the IG Joyce cartel, would choose to open an office in the Pynchon industry? Fortunately, the identification of a source in Pynchon does not lead in circular fashion to a curious bit of antiquariana that illuminates nothing outside the work or its literary tradition. Behind Pynchon stands Weber, whose concepts and vocabulary have articulated structures by which the world has actually been affected. Behind Joyce stands Victor Bérard, whose *Les Phéniciens et l'Odysée* is an interesting work of scholarly reconstruction but nothing more. And where Pynchon uses social, political, and economic systems which actually affect our lives, Joyce uses not even the historical illuminations of Bérard but the arbitrary speculations of Madame Blavatsky and the occult "sciences."

Pynchon, in choosing one aspect of the history of language to serve metonymically for the whole, selected the most inescapably political aspect he could find. The introduction of the NTA involves a complex of political motives arising in the decisions of a central authority, and shaped by political circumstances. When Joyce offers a history of language linked metaphorically to embryology, he implies that the development of language is entirely a natural process, its variety and change deriving from a process of evolution substantially unaffected by locality or motive. (Joyce's connection between language and its representative is a metaphoric not a metonymic one: relations in Joyce are analogical and aesthetic, in Pynchon etiological and historic.) For Pynchon, as for the rest of us, the separation of language from the world it alters and describes is not an unchanging ontological problem but a political one, whose recognition ultimately permits the possibility of voluntary action and response.

II

The political history of language in *Gravity's Rainbow* has antecedents in the accounts of statecraft that inform all encyclopedic narratives, whether explicitly as in Don Quixote's instructions for Sancho Panza's governorship, or by inversion as in the rules of the Abbey of Thélème or the decrees of the New Bloomusalem. Statecraft is a larger matter than social observation. Almost all novels, until recently at least, concern themselves not only with character but also with a descriptive account (in some cases prescriptive) of the specific society in which the characters live. Upon such description encyclopedic narrative superimposes a theory of social organization, normally a theory which offers itself implicitly for *use* outside the book. The writing of an encyclopedic narrative proves to be a political act, and the narrative itself tends sooner or later to be co-opted for political purposes—of which some, certainly, have been alien to the book's author. Dante's use of his native Tuscan in preference to international Latin had political consequences for Italian nationalism—or at least provided a focus for later political acts. In *Le Conflit des Interprétations,* Paul Ricoeur writes that the display of a world and the positioning of an ego are symmetrical and reciprocal. Encyclopedic narrative not only locates an ego, it also locates a culture or a nation.

Furthermore, the development of a nation's self-recognition, and its identification of an encyclopedic narrative or author as its central cultural monument, are also reciprocal processes. The idea of Italian or German nationality makes use of Dante or Goethe while at the same time canonizing them (in the original senses of the word). But encyclopedic narratives begin their history from a position *outside* the culture whose literary focus they become; they only gradually find a secure place in a national or critical order. Dante writes the *Commedia* in exile; Rabelais's books fall under the interdict of the Sorbonne, and their author has to go into hiding; Cervantes refers to *Don Quixote* as "just what might be begotten in a prison"; Goethe allows publication of Part II of *Faust* only after his death; *Moby-Dick* receives most of its early recognition in England; the last words printed in the encyclopedia of Dublin are "Trieste-Zürich-Paris." To an extent unknown among other works that have become cultural monuments, encyclopedic narratives begin their career *illegally*.

Short of committing a crime, there is little a modern writer in Western Europe or North America can do, as writer, to put himself in an illegal position. In any case, the illegality of encyclopedic narratives is never deliberately *sought* by their authors. The West's wide range of toleration leaves, paradoxically, only a narrow area for dissent—which Pynchon has managed to occupy. His elusive near-anonymity, which entirely predates his encyclopedic efforts, is a stance alien to our literary culture; and *Gravity's Rainbow*'s drastic violations of what remains of the tattered fabric of literary decorum assert a further distance from officialdom. Critics who praise Pynchon tend to gloss over the uncomfortable fact that he writes quite a few stomach-turning pages. Slothrop's nightmare of a descent through the sewers, Brigadier Pudding's coprophilia, Mexico and Bodine's verbal disruption of officialdom at the dinner table—or Mexico's urinary dissolution of the solemnity of an official meeting—are all gross violations of literary and social decorum. When critics blithely quote such passages, as if they were as innocuous as Longfellow, they do Pynchon a disservice in ignoring the uncomfortable fact that his language retains an unmistakable power to shock and disgust, without ever allowing itself to be dismissed as infantilism or mere noise. Only a false sophistication—or a terminally brutalized sensibility—can claim not to be repelled by many pages of *Gravity's Rainbow*.

The illegality of Pynchon's vision has already been illuminated by a critic who never heard of Pynchon: Mikhail Bakhtin in *Rabelais and His World*. Bakhtin provides the finest available introduction to the decorum of *Gravity's Rainbow*, and in consequence, demonstrates the deep historical roots of Pynchon's literary mode. Bakhtin observes that Rabelais's laughter stands assertively outside the realm of dogma and law, and that Rabelais writes at a moment when a received hierarchical system suffers the strains that will ultimately shatter it. Pynchon, like Rabelais, proposes a grotesquerie that governance can never acknowledge, a vital energy that officialdom must always seek to rationalize or destroy. Bakhtin's discussion of Rabelais's use of the common perception that urine has a power both debasing and generating brings Mexico's gesture of revolt in Mossmoon's office into sharper focus. Bakhtin's analysis of the use of excrement in the feast of fools rescues Katje's debasement of Brigadier Pudding from its narrow place in a catalogue of perversions, and allows it to serve as a vision of the temporary, but recurring, reversals that restore energy to the sullen bureaucracies of the rationalized world.

In a *positive,* or affirming, illegality Roger Mexico and Jessica Swanlake (whose first initials recall two earlier illegal lovers in Verona) enjoy their love only during the chaotic disorder of the war. They come together in forbidden territory, an evacuated village under barrage balloons. After the war, "in the rationalized power-ritual that will be the coming peace," Jessica will return to an empty legality, and lose "her cheeky indifference to death-institutions"; she "will take her husband's orders . . . will become a domestic bureaucrat." Wretched at his loss, Mexico resorts to *negative* illegality, gestures of revolt that save him from living within an empty legal order, but otherwise do little more than satisfy a nose-thumbing impulse, and establish no alternate enterprise of love or understanding. On a larger scale, the negative illegality of the book's black markets establishes false and betraying systems, whose agents and organizers end in blithering inanity. Tyrone Slothrop ends in a condition of *a*legality, neither in revolt against social organization, nor, certainly, in concord with it, but in absolute separation from all systems of organization whatever.

An encyclopedic narrative is a work of positive illegality, originating in moments of hierarchical strain and cultural distress. But some years after its author sends it out into the world, and after literary orthodoxy has expended much energy in attempting to exile or dismiss the book's outrageousness, the book itself, now safely settled in the literary-historical past, becomes an element in a centripetal network of official cultural self-consciousness and the focus of an organized bureaucracy of textual and historical scholarship. The cartels of Goethe G.m.b.H., Dante Internazionale S.A., and IG Joyce are continuing organizations, where specialization and the division of labor are (below certain high levels of management) well-observed procedures, in which recognized authorities deliver written verdicts on the work of lesser figures in the organization, and in which, more often than not, a position in the firm guarantees a lifetime of steady work and reliable remuneration. These are, of course, the characteristics Weber assigns to legal bureaucracies in general. And the process by which an encyclopedic narrative becomes integrated into its culture — becomes, in fact, the focus of an organized culture of its own — is a version of the pandemic Weberian process in *Gravity's Rainbow,* the process through which charismatic eruptions, originating in moments of cultural distress, become rationalized into legal bureaucracy.

Charisma, in Pynchon studies, is not only about to be rationalized, it is about to become a very tired subject indeed. It is not, however, Pynchon's only inheritance from Weber. Pynchon's pervasive insistence on the reality of *process* finds theoretical justification in Weber's social analyses, which pursue a dynamic understanding of society rather than a reified one. At a séance early in *Gravity's Rainbow,* the spirit of Walter Rathenau refers to the successions of geologic strata — "epoch on top of epoch, city on top of ruined city." "These signs are real,"

Rathenau (or Pynchon's extension of him) continues. "They are also symptoms of a process. The process follows the same form, the same structure. To apprehend it you will follow the signs. All talk of cause and effect is secular history, and secular history is a diversionary tactic." The signs we are to follow are only signs, but they are the shells and the consequence of sacred (not secular) processes: "Names by themselves may be empty, but the *act of naming* . . ." Pynchon's italics and evocative ellipsis).

Like the hieratic language of *The Crying of Lot 49*, Weberian processes and terminology invade even the smallest crevices in the texture of *Gravity's Rainbow*. When Mexico envisions Jessica as "a domestic bureaucrat," he echoes Weber, as does Squalidozzi in explaining the control of "the center" (Weber's Central Zone) in ordinary times. Blicero's carefully separated technicians, each with his function in the *Schwarzgerät* project, make up a textbook example of the division of labor. A universal obsession in *Gravity's Rainbow* is *control*, Pynchon's translation of Weber's *Herrschaft*. Weber distinguishes three pure types of authority or control, for each of which Pynchon provides a parody or a representation. The three types are *legal* domination, accomplished through a bureaucratic administrative staff (exemplified by "the Firm" and all the acronymic branches of the Allied war effort), *traditional* domination by patriarchies or by military leaderships with relatively independent surrogates (as in Tchitcherine's relation to Stalin), and *charismatic* authority centered on the exceptional qualities or powers of a leader's personality (as in Enzian's authority over the Schwarzkommando, an authority ultimately to be fulfilled "after" the end of the book, through his sacrificial ascension in the rocket).

Slothrop himself embodies a parody of charismatic authority that Weber never anticipated: the mock-charismatic figure entirely victimized by an authority he neither wants nor understands. Slothrop first distinguishes himself when it is noticed that a map he keeps of his sexual adventures (real or fantasized) corresponds in a statistically significant manner with a map of V-2 strikes on London. To make the matter more perplexing, the stars on Slothrop's map *precede* by a few days the stars on a map of rocket strikes. Slothrop eventually becomes aware of a relation between his sexual impulses and the V-2 rocket, but the *precise* nature and cause of that relation never emerges in the book, and it remains entirely a mystery. Pointsman, committed to the use of bureaucracy and the rationalized world of Pavlovian psychology, thinks Slothrop a "monster" whose continued subjugation to official *Herrschaft* is necessary for the maintenance of order in the large: "*We must never lose control.* The thought of him lost in the world of men, after the war, fills me with a deep dread I cannot extinguish" (the last word recalls Pavlov's "extinguishing" of conditioned reflexes). But Slothrop escapes into the chaos of the Zone. Weber emphasizes that charisma appears at times of political, economic, social, religious, and cultural distress (legal and traditional domination are adequate to ordinary times), and it is at the chaotic end of the war that Slothrop's mock-charisma becomes most manifest. In Berlin he tries on the costume of a Wagnerian tenor, and looks a bit like the V-2 rocket whose special (charismatic) qualities he has been seeking to identify. Those around him immediately call him Rocketman, and take for granted his attainment of the charismatic powers that belong to any comic-book hero: "No job is too tough for Rocketman." By mere accident Slothrop's presence manages to confound official-dom — without Slothrop even being aware of it — and he is elevated into a "force": "There is a counterforce in the Zone," Tchitcherine is convinced. Eventually Slothrop adopts the costume of the charismatic pig-hero of a German town. When Russian police enter a melee on the day of the annual celebration of the pig's heroic feats, Slothrop wonders if he is "expected to repel *real* foreign invaders now?"

Weber applies the term "charisma" to "a certain quality of an individual personality by virtue of which he is set apart from ordinary men and treated as endowed with supernatural, superhuman, or at least specifically exceptional powers or qualities." So far, this description fits Slothrop precisely, but Weber goes on to say that a charismatic figure, in consequence of his special powers, is "treated as a leader," as Slothrop decidedly is not. "The Schwarzgerät is no Grail, Ace. . . . And you no knightly hero." Far from being led by Slothrop, every official organization in Europe seems to think that he is the agent of their own interests. And the Counterforce that organizes around its desire to rescue him from dissolution becomes at last a bureaucracy committed to denying Slothrop's charismatic authority, not maintaining it: "We were never that concerned with Slothrop *qua* Slothrop."

Gravity's Rainbow, then, is *about* the rationalization of charismatic authority, but as an encyclopedic narrative, it is also the most recent member of a class of books that *enact* the same process in their own history. The process by which illegal charisma, originating in a moment of distress, becomes rationalized into legal bureaucratic organization, is precisely the process by which encyclopedic narrative, conceived outside the received systems of literary culture, becomes a central element in successor organizations, the focus of new bureaucracies. And so *Gravity's Rainbow* prophesies not only Western history between the time of its action and the time of its publication but also its own history, the history of its own reception.

III

From his position at the edge of a culture, an encyclopedist redefines that culture's sense of what it means to be human. An encyclopedic narrative prophesies the modes of human action and perception that its culture will later discover to be its own central concerns. The disturbing "illegal" strangeness of most encyclopedic narratives at the time of their publication, the differences between the book and its culture's self-conceptions, are the result of the encyclopedist's understanding of modes of meaning that a culture has already begun to use but has not yet learned to acknowledge.

It is the interior world that has dominated the most noteworthy sophisticated fiction in the English language during this century, and the most precisely detailed literary presentation of interior experience is its encyclopedia: Joyce's *Ulysses.* The assumptions made in *Ulysses* as to what is significant in the world of reality, and what is not, have become the generally unexamined assumptions in most British and American fiction during the past fifty years. *Ulysses* is in no way the cause of the depressingly universal acceptance of the assumptions it embodies, but its massive authority has given special sanction to the literary modes—many of them not at all "Joycean"—of which it is the most notable exemplar.

The emergence of a writer whose authority is comparable to Joyce's, but who breaks radically with Joyce's assumptions—as Mexico suggests to Pointsman that science must "have the courage to junk cause-and-effect entirely, and strike off at some other angle"—allows us to recognize that Joyce's perspective is a special one, without conclusive authority for the modern era. My point here is hardly to diminish Joyce: I hope instead that an account of his successor-encyclopedist will inevitably suggest ways in which both Joyce's and Pynchon's work may be *located* more accurately than criticism has been able to do until now. *Gravity's Rainbow* provides an encyclopedic presentation of the world from a perspective that permits inclusion of fields of data and realms of experience that Joyce's perspective excludes. To locate the perspectives of *Gravity's Rainbow* is to demonstrate the possibility of perspectives radically different from those of most modern fiction, yet allowing comparable or greater intellectual range, aesthetic amplitude, and emotional depth.

I will begin with a little-understood aspect of *Gravity's Rainbow* which is perhaps its single greatest technical achievement in the art of writing. Pynchon's characters live *in their work* and in their relations to large social and economic systems. (Hence the emphasis, early in the book, on the concept of the *interface*.) In *Gravity's Rainbow,* as in life, people think about the world in ways related to the work they do much of the day. Pynchon's sample of professions tends to be highly educated and specialized, but his sample is certainly less askew than Joyce's sampling of a Dublin where no one seems to do much work at all. (The only kinds of work observed in any detail in most modern literature are reflexive variations on the work of writers themselves: the "work" of psychiatrists, poets, or as in the case of Leopold Bloom, the advertising canvasser. The census bureau is correct in refusing to include in its list of job categories "forge in the smithy of my soul the uncreated conscience of my race.") We are accustomed to fictional characters whose work is all done "offstage," or in an office that is nothing but a backdrop for personal dramas that could take place anywhere, and we fail to notice that the elements chosen by a novelist for the presentation of such characters exclude an enormous segment of the data which, in our own daily lives, is essential to our knowledge of self and others. Joyce, who serves as the clearinghouse for the technical means of presenting character in modern fiction, saw no need to associate personality with work, and the older technical means of doing so have by now mostly been forgotten. Through a corollary of the modern prejudice that gives primacy to the affective aspects of personality, characters who live in their work tend to be dismissed by readers as "types," lacking in any substantial distinction or interest. All literary innovations are in part recoveries of lost techniques, and Pynchon's radical analysis of character includes recollections of such lost modes as the seventeenth-century developments of the Theophrastian character, and the allegorical type. But Pynchon modifies his recollection of older modes by acknowledging modern modes of psychological complexity (which he does not, however, place at the center of his presentation of character). Pynchon's world looks at first like a world we can never enter, a world lacking in the kind of people we know (or know about). But Pynchon knows more than his readers: eventually one realizes that the world which seems strange in Pynchon contains major elements of our own world that, although familiar to the language of politics and economics, have not yet adequately been named or assimilated in the language of fiction.

Pynchon signaled his redefinition of character in *The Crying of Lot 49*. There the name Oedipa refers not to the psychological permutations of the Oedipal complex but to the social and ethical convolutions of responsibility in which the Sophoclean Oedipus found himself implicated. So, in *Gravity's Rainbow*, character is defined not only by interior affective considerations but by action within a complex system of meanings — Weber's *Sinnzusammenhang* — which cannot be understood (as Freud understood society) to be merely a projection or extension of private categories and internal organizations.

Pynchon's vision of the world of politics is integral with his rendering of the nature of personality. His political world is made up of cartels, corporations, bureaucracies, multinational and historically extended systems that are larger than the personalities involved in them, and whose organization is independent of private concerns. Joyce is equally consistent in his politics and his psychology: the politics in *Ulysses*, for all its wealth of local detail, are effectively large projections of *family* politics. Anything more elaborate would violate the formulae of paternity around which the book is organized. But as a solution to the political problem of encyclopedic organization—precisely the organization that Joyce claimed for his book—it is far too naïve and inadequate for anyone except literary critics to take seriously. Joyce comforts with his comic vision of the human scale and human correlation of all things, Pynchon disturbs and rebukes with his insistence on the real power of forces too enormous for us to influence or too minuscule or too patient and slow for us to recognize.

On the surface, of course, Joyce's politics seem to have wisdom, rationality, and weight, while Pynchon's seem obsessive, aberrant, and crazed. But Pynchon, here as elsewhere, adheres to the law by which self-conscious narrative can admit serious meanings only through indirection. Knowing the limits of fiction's power to persuade—and its ethical responsibility *not* to persuade that a fiction can be sufficient to the truth of the world—Pynchon consistently alters a serious vision of society through the distorting lens of paranoia. Yet if you "correct" for this distortion as the brain corrects the inverted image on the retina, and as Pynchon's strictures on paranoia *insist* that the distortion be corrected—the book yields a complex, dynamic, and plausible account of the social world. But no matter how hard you try to correct for the apparently reasonable lens of paternity in *Ulysses* (paternity or its counterpart metempsychosis in Joyce corresponding to paranoia in Pynchon), you cannot produce a recognizable vision of the social world larger than the family. Joyce's lens, although it transmits detail with vivid accuracy, permanently alters the structure of the image of the world outside the book; Pynchon's only bends it temporarily.

Joyce's ideal reader is an insomniac who spends all his time reading Joyce. Although the opening chapters of *Ulysses* propose to correct the heroic formality of the *Odyssey* through the daily quiddities of Dublin, the later chapters turn obsessively inward, to their own structure and verbal display. Pynchon, far from trying to seduce his readers and critics into a permanent relation with his texts, constantly urges us to distrust the enveloping embrace of fiction—to *use* fiction to call attention to the knowledge we need for making choices in the world outside. Pynchon's distrust of texts has a long ancestry: encyclopedic narratives all exhibit a love-hate relation with other books. For all his admiration for Virgil, Dante knows that secular literature cannot lead him to a vision of Paradise. Cervantes blames Don Quixote's madness entirely on his confusion of the fictional excitement of the romances with the ethical requirements of the world. *Gravity's Rainbow* constantly offers similar counterexamples against its own fascinations: texts that offer themselves for a reader's cathexis but are emphatically not "the real Text."

The clearest example is The Book—always capitalized and bearing too sacred an aura for its seven owners ever to name—bought by Pointsman and company, and passed ritually among them. It bears, Pointsman supposes, a "terrible curse." The title of The Book never appears in *Gravity's Rainbow,* but it is Pavlov's second series of "Lectures on Conditioned Reflexes," *Conditioned Reflexes and Psychiatry* (1941). (The pervasive presence of this book in *Gravity's Rainbow* illuminates, among many other matters, Pointsman's attempt to have Slothrop castrated, the relation for Pavlov of social systems to physiological systems, and the relation of paranoia to "pathological inertness" of the kind displayed by Slothrop before he disintegrates.) This sacred object has, for Pointsman, the effect only of limiting his understanding, forcing his perception of extraordinary events into the sterile categories that Pavlov proposes. But Pointsman is not the only victim of too great a reliance on a text's version of reality. The Schwarzkommando who construct their own rocket, the successor to the charismatic V-2 that carried the Schwarzgerät, come to think of the rocket as a "Text," but a text that "seduced us while the real Text persisted, somewhere else, in its darkness, in our darkness." The Counterforce that fails to save Slothrop replaces him with a carefully numbered and organized "Book of Memorabilia." In *Gravity's Rainbow* films have the same seductive falseness as written texts. An erotic scene in *Alpdrücken* is the occasion for erotic impulses in the film's viewers, and the children conceived as a product of the film become reduced to fictional counters in the eyes of their parents (see the story of Ilse Pökler). Pynchon leaves Gerhardt von Göll immersed in the making of a film that he will never finish. Pynchon's own buffoonery, the puns and pie-throwing that occur whenever matters threaten to become too serious, is a way of insisting that *Gravity's Rainbow* not be confused, even locally, with the world it illuminates.

Slothrop's disintegration at the end of the book is accompanied by his own confusion between the events in his past and a "text" that transforms and — inadequately — interprets those events. Slothrop progressively forgets the particularity of his past, and replaces his memory of past events with garnish and crude comic-book versions of them. His disintegration of memory is not the work of those who oppose or betray him but is the consequence of his own betrayals, his own loss of interest in the world, his own failures to relate and connect. Near the beginning of the book, when he first meets Katje, his past is still with him: "It's the past that makes demands here." But when he has entered his isolation in the Zone, his sense that acts have consequences in time begins to diminish; he forgets that he exists in a realm of responsibility where relations extend into the past and future. With Bianca on the *Anubis,* "Sure he'll stay for a while, but eventually he'll go, and for this he is to be counted, after all, among the Zone's lost. . . . He creates a bureaucracy of departure . . . but coming back is something he's already forgotten about." What Slothrop no longer remembers is that his actions occur not for their own sake, or for his, but in a complex of meaning, a *Sinnzusammenhang* of ethical responsibility. The engineer Kurt Mondaugen postulates

Mondaugen's Law: "Personal density is directly proportional to temporal band-width." Separated by his own escape and his own empty freedom from an orig-nating past or a future to which he could be responsible, Slothrop can only diminish and disintegrate. As his "temporal bandwidth"—the degree to which he "dwell[s] in the past and in the future"—diminishes, so must all his relations to the world.

When he forgets the world to which, if he could exist coherently, he would be somehow related, he does so by replacing his recollections with a text derived from popular culture. Slothrop himself has recognized that responsibility depends on memory and knowledge: when Säure Bummer makes a remark that reminds him of the Berkshire of his childhood, he decides that Bummer "can't possibly be on the Bad Guys' side. Whoever They are, Their game has been to extinguish, not remind." "They," everyone for whom Slothrop is a convenient victim, try to extinguish different elements of his mental structure: Jamf extin-guished the conditioned reflex of "infant Tyrone" twenty years before; Points-man, in trying to have Slothrop castrated, hopes to extinguish his mysterious relation to the rocket. But the only extinguishing that succeeds is Slothrop's own increasing inability to remember who and where he is. Near the end of the book, Slothrop, already "corrupted," yields the remnants of his memory to patterns picked up from the comic books. In a long passage set in Slothrop's comic-book construction of the Raketen-Stadt, he thinks of his relation to his parents in terms of a fantasy of the Floundering Four *vs.* Pernicious Pop and his Parental Peril. Finally, his disintegration all but complete, he can remember neither his parents nor even the etiolated images that have supplanted them.

Gravity's Rainbow has on occasion been misunderstood as an endorsement of popular culture in preference to "high" culture, but Pynchon is equally insis-tent on the potential dangers that lie in absorption at either extreme. The pop-ular modes that Pynchon assimilates into his encyclopedia of styles are never modes of liberation from the systems of oppression but are instead a *means* of op-pression and extinguishing. In his references to popular forms, Pynchon inci-dentally commits historical errors of a kind absent from his allusions to Rossini or Rilke: he is not, for example, sufficiently interested in a film like *The Return of Jack Slade* to notice that its inclusion in *Gravity's Rainbow* is a ten-year anachronism.

IV

Gravity's Rainbow is a book that recalls origins and foresees endings, but it insists on the continuing responsibility of those who live in the present that lies between. Its attention to charisma is necessarily a concern with origins, for, in Weber, charisma in its pure form exists only in the process of originating. It cannot remain stable. *Gravity's Rainbow* explores a variety of originating moments, most vividly that of the rocket's ascent "on a promise, a prophecy of Escape" from the distress that gives rise to charisma. But the ascent, "betrayed to Gravity," leads nowhere but to a dead end. Only during its originating moments of ascent does it appear to have a fiery "life," and only then can its direction be altered, through telemetry, by human control or *Herrschaft*. After its engine stops, the rocket becomes a piece of inanimate junk, its course irrevocably determined. *Gravity's Rainbow* perceives the contemporary era in terms of its first brief moments of origination and possibility, when the means of control, Pynchon suggests, were engaged and the political and technological character of our time determined once and for all.

Yet the book insists that we are not determined, as the inanimate rocket is determined, unless, paradoxically, we *choose* to be, by submitting to Pavlovian brain-mechanics or to the hopeless linkages of cause and effect. The possibilities of freedom, the whole range of probabilities that lie between and outside the one and the zero, exist in the book but are always difficult to locate or achieve. Everyone in *Gravity's Rainbow* who confronts the agonies of choice and decision tries to dream instead of a world in which all difficulties of choice are removed—in which the condition of the world has miraculously been altered for the better—in which an illusory and easy "freedom" *from* the problems of responsibility and the anxiety of human limitation somehow replaces the true and difficult freedom *to* act and choose. Enzian dreams that "Somewhere, among the wastes of the World, is the key that will bring us back, restore us to our Earth and to our freedom," or that there might be "an Aether sea to bear us world-to-world [to] bring us back a continuity, show us a kinder universe." And Slothrop imagines that "somewhere in the waste" of the disordered Zone might be "a single set of coordinates from which to proceed, without elect, without preterite, without even nationality."

But these are exiles' fantasies of Eden and Utopia, evasions of responsibility in the immediate world of time. Faced with responsibility, Pynchon's characters can choose either to escape it in voluntary servitude to legal authority or the authority of a text, or to enact it, through free relations with others. Free relations are built on language, but language in Pynchon is the means of both freedom and oppression (as metaphor in *The Crying of Lot 49* is both "a thrust at truth and a lie"—*Lot 49*). In *The Crying of Lot 49* Oedipa's discovery of the positive illegality of the Tristero postal system is the means by which she achieves the possibility of vital and unfamilar relations that she may freely enter. In *Gravity's Rainbow,* where conditions are more difficult, the affirmative and "true" aspects of communications cluster, like almost all the book's moments of hope and love, around the character of Roger Mexico. (In this drug-ridden book, marked throughout with sexual cruelty and betrayal, it is Roger Mexico who never even lights a cigarette—the nicotine on his teeth at one point in the narrative is only in Bodine's imagination—who is neither sadist nor masochist, and who betrays no one. The day after Christmas 1944, Mexico realizes that his love for Jessica has broken down the barriers of self and even the language of self. He thinks:

> I'm no longer sure which of all the words, images, dreams or ghosts are "yours" and which are "mine." It's past sorting out. We're both becoming someone new now.

Immediately the narrator identifies Mexico's feelings in a charged phrase: they are "His act of faith." And in the next sentence the children in the street are singing:

> Hark the herald angels sing:
> Mrs. Simpson's pinched our King.

What is this topical carol doing here? The events of the abdication, to which it refers, occurred eight years earlier. Yet its juxtaposition to Mexico's uncertainty over what is "mine" or "yours" makes a specific point. This fractured carol is used by Iona and Peter Opie, near the opening of their classic book *The Lore and Language of Schoolchildren,* to illustrate the possibility of communication in a manner "little short of miraculous." The children's version of the carol, which could not have been broadcast or printed or repeated in music halls, managed to spread across all of England in the course of a few weeks, during school term, when there could have been little traveling that might speed its oral transmission. The children singing the verses could have no idea that they were enacting what *The Crying of Lot 49* calls the "secular miracle of communication."

But in other manifestations, communication can dislocate and destroy. The network of cartels that maintains observations on Slothrop is one whose activities are neither edifying nor miraculous. Among the varieties of connectedness in the world of *Gravity's Rainbow,* the connected communications of cartels and black markets are always profitable, but they are false. And the mechanist science that, in league with the empty legality of the Firm, hopes to eliminate hope, is a limited and false science that ultimately fails (as Pointsman, following his narrow logic, becomes "an ex-scientist now, one who'll never get Into It far enough to talk about God . . . left only with Cause and Effect and the rest of his sterile armamentarium." The true and vitalizing connectedness of sympathy and memory is always fragile. The quantum leap that Mexico must make to achieve his "act of faith" is a dangerous one, but only through vulnerability and risk can the book's true relations be achieved.

As all of Pynchon's books implicate their readers in the processes they describe, so *Gravity's Rainbow* invites its readers to make quantum leaps towards relationship in the very act of reading. *The Crying of Lot 49,* which is short enough to read at a sitting and hold in one's memory, allows its reader to make the unique binary choice of finding in the book either relation and indicative meaning, or chaos and subjunctive fantasy. But *Gravity's Rainbow* is far too large and complex for any adequate unified response. The zero / one choice available—demanded—in *Lot 49* is transformed, in the wider field of *Gravity's Rainbow,* to its empty opposite: the limiting matrix of Pointsman's Pavlovian brain-mechanics in which a stimulus produces either a response or none, and in which any issue that cannot be reduced to the control of binary notation is not worthy of attention. To read the encyclopedic *Gravity's Rainbow* is, necessarily, to read *among* the various probable interpretations of the book. There is no unavoidable choice to be found among the various networks of *Gravity's Rainbow,* but there are many varieties of probable relationships along which to find your way. Pynchon expounds the matter with reference, once again, to Roger Mexico:

> If ever the Antipointsman existed, Roger Mexico is the man. . . .
> [I]n the domain of zero to one, not-something to something, Points-
> man can only possess the zero and the one. He cannot, like Mexico,
> survive anyplace in between. Like his master I.P. Pavlov before him,
> [Pointsman] imagines the cortex of the brain as a mosaic of tiny on /
> off elements. . . . But to Mexico belongs the domain *between* the
> zero and the one—the middle Pointsman has excluded from his per-
> suasion—the probabilities.

(Incidentally, the transformation of binary choice, from the vitalizing choice of *Lot 49* to the restrictive mechanism of *Gravity's Rainbow,* continues Pynchon's procedure of inverting his central metaphors from one book to the next. In *V.* thermodynamic entropy increases, to the detriment of the world; while in *Lot 49* it is information entropy that increases, to the enrichment of those who live in the world.)

But there is a warning in this praise of Mexico, as well as encouragement. To know the probabilities is not necessarily to act on them. At the beginning of the book, for example, Mexico has not yet learned to recognize the full consequence of actions—see his exchange with Paul de la Nuit on sacrality and the *use* of probabilities—but he will learn. Mere understanding is inadequate to action—as art is not enough.

For although Mexico and the Counterforce of which he is a part achieve some understanding of the world-processes that affect their lives, they are finally unable or unwilling to do very much about it. Knowledge alone insures neither courage nor triumph. The Counterforce fails: "They are as schizoid, as double-minded in the massive presence of money, as any of the rest of us, and that's the hard fact. The Man has a branch office in each of our brains, his corporate emblem is a white albatross, each local rep has a cover known as the Ego. . . . We do know what's going on and we let it go on." Faced with the knowledge of "Their" power, Mexico is free to choose, but his choice is, by necessity, between life as "Their pet" and defiance leading to death. "It is not a question he has ever imagined himself asking seriously. It has come by surprise, but there's no sending it away now, for he really does have to decide. . . . Letting it sit for a while is no compromise, but a decision to live, on Their terms."

The solution—and there does prove to be a solution—to this tragic choice is a comic disruption of "Their" necessity, as Mexico and his ally, Seaman Bodine, disrupt the most official of dinner parties with the most nauseous and unofficial language. They escape unharmed because they have wrenched the realm of language away from its official manipulators, the western counterparts of the makers of the NTA, and have brought to the surface the unrationalizable physical disorder and illegal energy that officialdom keeps under restraint. Their use of language cannot alter the world, but it can save them for another battle. After this scene, Mexico disappears from the book.

Gravity's Rainbow's knowledge of language is encyclopedic and deep, but it insists that language is not all. The kill-the-police-commissioner sign in central Asia erupts out of the closed and static world of written "signs" into the world of irreversible acts, the world of life and death. To insist that language is separate from the world of acts (or, more subtly, that the world of acts consists only of linguistic acts) is to keep language at a safe distance from our lives. The worst, most dangerous moments in *Gravity's Rainbow* are the moments when words *act* on the world, when they are translated into lethal action. In a sequence set in Peenemünde, when Slothrop and others are in a dispute with some Russian soldiers, the narrator interrupts the action with this extraordinary address to Slothrop, to the reader, and to himself:

> But . . . what might that have been just now, waiting in this broken moonlight, camouflage paint from fins to point crazed into jigsaw . . . is it, then, really never to find you again? Not even in your worst times of night, with pencil words on your page only Δt from the things they stand for? And inside the victim is twitching, fingering beads, touching wood, avoiding any Operational Word. Will it really never come to take you, now?

So Slothrop, searching for the rocket ("fins to point") as if for the Grail, will never again be found *by* it—as all true searchers and authentic goals find and are found—not even at the "worst times of night" when words and things are separated infinitesimally, not in space but in *time,* by an unimaginably small time differential (delta-t). For Slothrop, living in a chaos of vacancy and dissociation, words and things will never find each other again. For the rest of us, the relation of words and things is often terrifying but is crucial to our lives. Our most difficult and vertiginous moments can be those when our words of hatred or love change the vulnerable lives of others and ourselves, when the words of others permanently alter our own knowledge and identity. In those moments events are separated by only the smallest gap, the smallest delta-t, from words; and those words—we sense with some relief—immediately fall away into the safety and permanence of memory or writing. The rocket's sacrificial victim avoids Words that Operate, words that have immediate effect, for when words act on the world, when the last delta-t is crossed, they have sufficient power to cause the direst of consequences. But Slothrop is no longer vulnerable even to words. His difficulty, predicted in this passage, is his eventual dissociation from *all* systems in which words have effect, or could have effect. The victim, in the rocket, is in the dangerous position where his words *can* have an effect—and a fatal one. But Slothrop, denied even the dignity of sacrifice, will be reduced to a fictional world of comic-book images and kabbalistic elaboration in which words are fluid and meanings arbitrary, where Slothrop will lose all real and potential relation to *any* world, whether of language or of act.

Moments of distress and disorder, uncrossable interfaces of delta-t, such as the dissolution of Germany or the scattering of Slothrop, are only temporary. States and bureaucracies immediately fill the disordered void. The charismatic ascent of a Gottfried or an Enzian is succeeded by the bureaucracy of the rocket cartel. The mock-charisma of Slothrop generates the system of the Counterforce, and Slothrop's dissolution is simultaneous with "his time's assembly." The world is never finally altered—and all is never gained nor lost. Total annihilation occurs only at the end of time. Within the world of time we know, there are crises and transformations, but total cataclysm cannot occur. In *Gravity's Rainbow,* as always in fiction, the devil has the best lines: it is Wernher von Braun who opens the book by asserting his conviction that "nature does not know extinction; all it knows is transformation."

Yet *Gravity's Rainbow* is, in a profound sense, a book about endings as well as about charismatic origins. Like William Slothrop, going westward in Imperial style, the book moves westward, in the direction of endings, the direction of the tragic necessity of the *Abendland*'s decline. Slothrop's dream of Crutchfield the westwardman resonates against the book's westward vision of the next war, whose first bomb explodes over the western city of Los Angeles. The final pages of the book rush forwards towards the west and towards endings, but almost simultaneously, the book rushes backwards through time, and eastwards through space, to Abraham and Isaac and the Judaic origins of the civilization of the west. In the last pages of the book "we" sit in the Los Angeles theatre on which the rocket is about to fall—as it "reaches its last unmeasurable gap above the roof of this old theatre, the last delta-t." But the final ending is delayed: "there is time" to sing William Slothrop's forgotten hymn, now miraculously remembered, as the hymn itself recalls the "light that hath brought the Towers low," and all the Preterite of "our crippl'd Zone." And the hymn anticipates the ultimate cataclysm that has not arrived, the end of things in the parousia, when the transfigured world will bear "a face on ev'ry mountainside, / And a soul in ev'ry stone."

But the book only anticipates this last postponed transfiguration. For us, as readers, nothing has changed. The book's prediction of the eschaton is a metaphor of its own ending: for us, all that has been concluded is our reading of a book. The last delta-t is not crossed by fiction. The rocket falls *after* the book's last words, outside the book's world. And within that world, where all events exist simultaneously in written words now unaffected by time, we find evidence that we have survived the explosion. The book's first sentence reads, "A screaming comes across the sky." If we have heard the rocket, we are safe: the sound that reaches us follows a destruction elsewhere. So, as readers, destruction has passed over us, and we have survived. But we have more of the knowledge that is required if we are to act freely outside the world of writing—in the world where acts have consequences, time is real, and our safety is far from certain.

Paranoia, Pynchon, and Preterition

Louis Mackey

> *God gave Noah the rainbow sign.*
> *No more water, the fire next time!*
> —Spiritual

> *God wasn't too bad a novelist, except he was a Realist.*
> —JOHN BARTH

One of Pynchon's characters remarks that there are only two kinds of people: paranoids and positivists. The positivists believe that things just happen, more or less at random. The paranoids are certain that everything is connected (though the connection cannot be seen) and that They have a plan (though you cannot know what it is). The paranoid's faith — his substance of things hoped for and his evidence of things not seen — is: someone's out to get me.

A positivist could not write a novel, not even (what *Gravity's Rainbow* almost was) a book of "mindless pleasures." The act of writing would impose and so dissimulate the very connectedness and order that the positivist ex professo is bound to deny. Novels don't just happen at random. They can only be made to seem to.

The paranoid can't exactly write a novel either. But he might conspicuously fail to write the novel that (perhaps) lurks like a spectre behind the grotesque facade of *Gravity's Rainbow.*

Along the story of Tyrone Slothrop's vacation adventures at the Casino Hermann Goering someone has strung out four "proverbs for paranoids." Here they are, foax, all together:

1. "You may never get to touch the Master, but you can tickle his creatures."

From *Sub-Stance,* no. 30 (Winter 1981). © 1981 by Sub-Stance, Inc.

2. "The innocence of the creatures is in inverse proportion to the immorality of the Master."

(How's that? The greater the immorality of the Master, the less the innocence of the creatures? And vice versa? Shouldn't it be the other way around? Proverb 3 replies—or does something—to these questions.)

3. "If they can get you asking the wrong question, they don't have to worry about the answers."

And 4. "*You* hide, they seek."

As Lt. Slothrop reflects one day in the Zone, when he finds that his faith is faltering (he's "losing his mind" actually):

> If there is something comforting—religious, if you want—about paranoia, there is still also anti-paranoia, where nothing is connected to anything, a condition not many of us can bear for long. . . . Either *They* have put him here for a reason, or he's just here. He isn't sure that he wouldn't, actually, rather have that *reason.*

And here's that Slothrop again, in another of his almost ubiquitous desperate straits—Slothrop de profundis: "Providence, hey Providence, what'd you do, step out for a beer or something?"

At Swinemünde the black-market impressario Gerhard von Göll observes with satisfaction that the ranks of the starving are dwindling day by day. When Slothrop objects ("that's a shitty thing to say"), Der Springer comes back like a prophet:

> Be compassionate. But don't make up fantasies about them. Despise me, exalt them, but remember, we define each other. Elite and preterite, we move through a cosmic design of darkness and light, and in all humility, I am one of the very few who can comprehend it *in toto.* Consider honestly, therefore, young man, which side you would rather be on. While they suffer in perpetual shadows, it's . . . always—

and he segues into the fox-trot, "Bright Days for the Black Market."

The paranoia that infests *Gravity's Rainbow* is manifestly a religious attitude. In fact a familiar religious attitude, just as American as apple pie and growing up absurd. Paranoia is described at one point as "a Puritan reflex . . . seeking other orders behind the visible." It is that paradoxical and singularly self-satisfied conjunction of total depravity and radical innocence that made this country great: old-fashioned New England Calvinism.

The heart of Calvinism is the doctrine of double predestination. God, whose absolute sovereignty Calvinists guarded more jealously than any Christians before them, has from all eternity relentlessly elected to save a few out of the corrupt mass of fallen humanity. The rest he passes over and allows to fall into hell borne down by the weight of Adam's and their own sin. All men are either Elect, the handful chosen for salvation, or Preterite, passed over and tacitly consigned to damnation.

In *Gravity's Rainbow* we see the divine decree of predestination from a new angle. All of our standard accounts were written by men persuaded of their own election. For all his agonized self-scrutiny, and in spite of his extraordinary bad luck with women (he is appropriately the opposite of Tyrone Slothrop in this respect), Sam Sewall never seriously doubted his eventual salvation. But in *Gravity's Rainbow* we are treated to the view from below. The Elect experience their election as the consciousness that all things, even tribulations, conspire together for their good. For the Preterite this converts to the strong suspicion, bordering on conviction, that "they're out to get me."

The Elite apprehend their privilege by faith. No certainty, it insinuates itself in occasional or recurrent signs of grace that order their otherwise unraveling lives. The plan is not clearly discerned, but it makes itself felt. Paranoia, which is just the will of God as perceived by the Preterite, is likewise an act of faith, nourished by disparate but distressingly almost-consistent signs of impending destruction. As the Elect may not be certain of their election, but nonetheless hope for tokens of the divine favor, so the paranoid does not know what the events of his life mean, whence that meaning accrues to them, or what he is being used for; but he senses just the same that his life is plotted and that all his actions are rigged. Not that he has proof. Positivistic counterexamples abound, suggesting that events occur with no particular rhyme or reason. But though the evidence is not conclusive—no unambiguous pattern evolves—it is nevertheless overwhelming. And so the paranoid hopes—or fears, often he doesn't know which—that all things are connected, that They do have a plan, and that his doom is sure.

Tyrone Slothrop's ancestor William published a book defending the view that grace had always been on the side of the Preterite. The System got him for that: the Boston theocracy burned his book and drove him out of the New Jerusalem. Which figures. Grace is gratuitous, that is, not part of the plan, therefore irrational and reprobate. Mad, like paranoia.

The action of *Gravity's Rainbow* begins (with a dream of death and resurrection) during Advent of 1944 and ends (with the passion of Gottfried) at the time of the autumnal—or is it the vernal?—sacrifice in 1945, after Slothrop, a kind of comical *pharmakos,* has been dismembered and dispersed. It may be that Pynchon's manifold paranoid blasphemies, like those of *his* ancestor William, who was also banned in Massachusetts, contrive a pious inversion of Calvinist

Christianity. As he explains to Karl Marx, "Christian Europe was always death, Karl, death and repression." Had America followed the Slothropite heresy, its history might have been life and liberation instead: "fewer crimes in the name of Jesus and more mercy in the name of Judas Iscariot."

But, as Richard M. Nixon once said, let me make one thing perfectly clear. When I say that paranoia is a religious attitude, I am not trying to suck edification from sour pickles. I merely observe that the *shape* of piety is always the same, whether it be the piety of the Elect or the piety of the Preterite.

The piety of the Preterite merits further refinement. The first discrimination in the divine decrees is between Elect and Reprobate. But some writers subdivide the Reprobate. There are the Reprobate in the strict sense, whom God designates for damnation. And there are the Preterite, whom he passes over and does not sign either for salvation or perdition, but who are of course damned anyway by the inertia of sin. All men are drowning. A few of them God mercifully plucks out of the water and revives. Some are pushed down and held under. The rest are allowed to sink on their own. A seventeenth-century theologian distinguished the positive act of punishment from the privative act of preterition, both of which he ascribed to God's simple prescience. A writer of the late nineteenth century spoke of "the reprobates who are damned because they were always meant to be damned, and the preterite who are damned because they were never meant to be saved."

That would appear to be a disconsoling precision for the Preterite. As the name implies, they participate inversely in the eternal decrees: they are included only as omitted. Negatively prehended by God, they go their way to an end that is just as ineluctable and just as desolate as the damnation of the Reprobate. Maybe more so, since it is not distinguished by divine notice. Deprived of the dignity imparted by God's individuating wrath, the Preterite perish en masse in His ignorance.

Gravity's Rainbow is set among the Preterite, the "second sheep," "out of luck and out of time." Each of them hears a voice speaking only to him and saying, "You didn't really believe you'd be saved. Come, we all know who we are by now. No one was ever going to take the trouble to save *you*, old fellow."

Tyrone Slothrop, descended from an ancient line of American Puritans, finally escapes the clutches of "shit, money, and *the Word,* the three American truths" (my emphasis) and rejoins his earliest New England ancestor on the side of the Preterite. "*They*" chose him — or so this paranoid sometimes believes — "because of all those *word-smitten Puritans* dangling off [his] family tree" (my emphasis). He was sent into the Zone to be present at his own assembly — "perhaps, heavily paranoid voices have whispered, *his time's assembly*." But the plan went wrong, and he is broken down and scattered instead. Everyone loses sight of him. Analyst Mickey Wuxtry-Wuxtry explains that the villainous Laszlo Jamf was only a fiction to help Slothrop explain his erotic fascination with death. "These early Americans," he says, "were a fascinating combination of crude poet and psychic cripple." The spokesman for the Counterforce admits (lies?) to *The Wall Street Journal,* "We were never concerned with Slothrop *qua* Slothrop." He was only a pretext . . . or perhaps a point-for-point microcosm.

By the end of the book Seaman Pig Bodine is the only person who can still perceive Slothrop as an integral creature. No one else can even imagine him. As they put it, "It's just got too remote." There is what may be a snapshot of him on the only album ever released by an English rock group called "The Fool." One of the faces in the group might be his—no none knows for sure if or which —and "the only printed credit that might apply to him is 'Harmonica, kazoo—a friend.'" The narrative continues, "But knowing his Tarot, we would expect to look among the Humility, among the gray and preterite souls, to look for him adrift."

Late in the story we are given bits and pieces of Slothrop's Tarot reading. All of his hopeful cards are reversed, especially and most woefully the Hanged Man, who upright (that is, upside down) represents "wisdom, circumspection, discernment, trials, sacrifice, intuition, divination, prophecy," but reversed (upright) signifies "selfishness, the crowd, body politic." His significator is covered by the 3 of Pentacles reversed, which means:

> a long and scuffling future . . . , mediocrity (not only in his life but also, heh, heh, in his chroniclers too, yes yes nothing like getting the 3 of Pentacles upside down covering the significator on the second try to send you to the tube to watch a seventh rerun of the Takeshi and Ichizo show . . .) . . . no clear happiness or redeeming cataclysm.

00000

I have laid a lot of words on the theological meaning of preterition. Which was inevitable under the circumstances. That's the first order of preterition in *Gravity's Rainbow,* and there are pages (roughly 760) of examples. But it's only the first order. Tyrone Slothrop is preterite not only in his destiny but also (heh, heh) in his chronicler. Back to the tube for the seventh rerun of a vulgar Kamikase sitcom, he himself ends as a motley of pop signifiers. Was he ever more than that?

The second order of preterition devolves from the further meanings of the word. Preterite, which means "passed over," also means just "past." As Webster puts it, with exquisitely unconscious paranoid sensitivity, "a verb tense that indicates action in the past without reference to duration, continuance, or repetition."

Restored to its native Latin, *praeteritio* identifies a figure of rhetoric. The Greek *paraleipsis,* the figure of conspicuous omission. Omission by mention, or mention by omission.

At the level of its rhetoric *Gravity's Rainbow* is a sustained piece of preterition. It displays on its rhetorical surface a linguistic paranoia which answers to the "deep" paranoia of its plots and personae. That is, by preterition (passing over) it constructs them as preterite (past). What is conspicuously omitted is perspicuously obscured.

Some details, at random and of unequal importance: in the main plot involving Slothrop and the Rocket, a number of clues are planted, the meanings of which would clear up for once and for all the significance of the Rocket itself and of Slothrop's erotic connection with the Rocket. But the meanings are not given. Though a number of imperfectly paranoid critics have been eager to help us out, we never learn what the *Schwarzgerät* is, what the "mystery stimulus" was that occasioned Slothrop's V-2 related hard-ons, what the Kirghiz Light is, and so on through a whole string of crucial and critically mislaid identities. Identities which function in the fiction not in spite of but precisely because of and in proportion to their elusive and spectral character.

Here's an instance of greater magnitude. *Gravity's Rainbow* is obsessed with death. And yet deaths (singular deaths, terminations, fulfillments) are not narrated. They are sometimes reported after they happen: the death of Tantivy Mucker-Maffick, mass deaths in the concentration camps and in German Southwest Africa, the extinction of the Dodo. Bianca's death (on a ship named *Anubis,* which means "death") is horribly suggested, but it happens — if that *is* what happened — during Slothrop's (and the narrator's) absence from the scene. It is certain that Gottfried will die as the rocket moves through *Brennschluss* and turns downward in its predestined course. But "the exact moment of his death will never be known."

The one death for which we are most exquisitely prepared never comes off. We witness Klaus Närrisch awaiting his certain end at the hands of the Russians, meditating the last moments of John Dillinger, fingering his machine gun, and reflecting that tomorrow he will not have to worry about the blisters on his fingers. He's a goner for sure. Almost fifty pages later he turns up again, in the hands of the Russians, full of sodium amytal and babbling to Tchitcherine the secrets of the *S-Gerät* and the *Fünffachnullpunkt.*

These deaths are all preteritions. Including those that don't happen, for the survivors are just as preterite as the slain. The Schwarzkommando who escaped von Trotha's campaign console themselves with the Herero mantra "Mba-kayere," which means, "I am passed over." Preterition *can* mean survival. And yet these deaths, like the lives they do not take, are emphatically not culminations, endings that give meaning to what has passed. Of none of them could it be said, *consummatum est*. And still the dead haunt the story. Pynchon's nonnarration of death intimidates by its absence. Death is everywhere at hand (the War), repeatedly recollected (the several cases of genocide past), and always imminent ("Now everybody—"). But it is not narratively experienced. It is always only the unnameable object of a paranoid faith, most real and most terrifying because it is not told. The narrative distancing of death, itself a preterition, is a preterition of the second order.

More important than these quasi-substantives, the linguistic texture of *Gravity's Rainbow* has bothered some readers with its apparent disdain for all the norms and conventions of "literature." Almost the entire story is told in the crudest kind of 1940s pop talk. The metaphors of this talk are the popular media: the movies, TV, comic strips, advertising slogans. Pornography. Drug lore. And popular song: like a cheap musical, *Gravity's Rainbow* lapses into song at the most inopportune moments. The language is pretty consistently vulgar. The names of the characters are glaringly "meaningful," often suggesting obscenity. Not to mention the overt and frequently deviant obscenity. And Pynchon never passes up an opportunity—he'll make one if he has to—for a horrible pun. "For De Mille, young fur-henchmen can't be rowing!" Did we really need that?

Pynchon has insisted—consciously, if not all-too-consciously—on taking an abysmal tone in what is—obviously, if not all-too-obviously—a serious text dealing with lofty themes. Even when the rhetoric does become exalted, as in Roger's and Jessica's poignant Advent service or the pathetic story of the Pöklers, the swell and expansion of the language is periodically checked and deflated by intrusions of Pynchon's more typical slang. Every ingredient of form—myth, symbol, archetype, history, allegory, romantic quest, even the ritual sanctities of science—is framed and qualified by the underslung tone of the narrative voice.

The blatantly low style of *Gravity's Rainbow* is a rhetorical way of searching among the humility and the preterite for a form suitably inappropriate to its content. Not quite the *sermo humilis* of early Christian stylistics, Pynchon's linguistic posturing is what one critic has described as "undergraduate defenses against seriousness . . . part of a more terrible seriousness." An embarrassed and self-conscious way of talking about grave and momentous things, and a preterition of sorts. There is no matching of style to theme and no assertion of an incarnational realization of the noble in the vulgar (as in *sermo humilis*) but rather a discrepancy that implies the solemnity of the matter only negatively by means of the gross incompetence of the manner.

The language of *Gravity's Rainbow* refuses to take itself and its powers seriously. It is deliberately not literary, where "literary" stands for the romantic (and late romantic modernist) conception of a language perfectly integrated in itself and perfectly comprehensive of its meaning. *Gravity's Rainbow* does not wish to be a self-referring and self-obsessed structure that contains all its expresses. On the contrary, it is open with an artfully naïve openness. Self-wounded, it is therefore vulnerable by all the canons of good taste. Not because Pynchon, poor fellow, simply cannot write like a proper author. His occasional "elevated" passages proscribe that conclusion. He has willfully produced a text insufficiently sophisticated to build and maintain its own defenses. A text that rejects literary propriety with all its presuppositions, so that it seems adolescent and a bit shamed by its own self-exposure. A-and, it literally stutters.

Pynchon's book bombards us with data, tempts us with a surfeit of clues. But the data never entail a sure conclusion, and the clues lead not to solutions but to further problems: "this is not a disentanglement from, but a progressive *knotting into.*" There are signs — too many signs — but nothing assuredly signified; a jumble of texts but no reliable edition. Lots of noise and little information. The language — this is the secret of its mastery — is not master of itself. It has renounced self-mastery, so that there is no "authentic" text of *Gravity's Rainbow.* All the questions it broaches are over-researched, over-documented, and left in the breach. Whatever it says garrulously and disconcertingly fails to make the point. And that of course is the point. The power of Pynchon's language is its self-dissipation. Its energy is expended in verbal waste and degradation. "Th' expense of spirit in a waste of shame. . . ." Like that intricately orchestrated orgy on board the *Anubis* which ends in a communal orgasm, it achieves the bad infinite: the ouroboric state of perfect entropy. You may never get to touch the Master, but you can tickle his creatures to death. Or to exhaustion, which is the same thing.

The paranoid — it figures — can't win. He is doomed either to destruction or to dissolution. One or the other. Destruction if his paranoid faith (that is, fear) is warranted, dissolution if his anti-paranoid hope (that is, anxiety) is confirmed. He opts for verbal dissolution — the opposite of that verbal integration which is supposed to define literary language — and in so doing negatively adumbrates his destruction. But it's always an open question. Perversely nonliterary language is the refusal of closure. And the suicide of the song, *Sold on Suicide,* is indefinitely postponed through what cannot ever, thanks to Gödel's theorem, become a complete catalogue of renunciations.

What is the plot, or what are the plots, of *Gravity's Rainbow?* The interlacings and interfacings of the plots in the fictional sense (the sort of thing Aristotle might have recognized had he first read Sterne) are repeatedly — we could say "deliberately," but we don't dare — confused with Plot in the sense that only a paranoid would understand. The plotting — *mimesis praxeos* as well as conspiracy — seems to be forged, in both senses of that word. It occurs (or does not occur) outside the narrative sequence and provides no clear index to narratorial intention. "Paranoia allows plot — is plot. But to carry the pun that far is to turn narrative into madness." Exactly.

Gravity's Rainbow is told by an omniscient narrator. At least it's not first person, stream of consciousness, epistolary narration, a narrative distributed among several voices, or any of the other familiar techniques. But this narrator does everything in his power to make us doubt the omniscience formally implied by his assumption of the role. Almost every word he utters undermines our confidence in his ability to handle this thing. He is no more in control of his story than he is in charge of what it darkly forbodes. It is not obvious that he is even a single persona, since his relationship to his story is continually changing. Narrative point of view and narrator affect vary from episode to episode, page to page. Sometimes he is the detached ironic observer, sometimes he is sympathetically within his characters sharing their passions. Sometimes he's frivolous, sometimes grave, and as a rule each mood is interrupted by the other. Anticipating the disintegration of Tyrone Slothrop, the narrator himself is fragmented and dispersed into his characters, for whom often (but not always) he speaks. Like them, he is not well-rounded. And much less reliable.

Pynchon's narrator doesn't answer the questions he raises. Sometimes he passes them to the reader: "Is the baby smiling, or is it just gas? Which do you want it to be?" Every once in a while he makes it painfully clear that his story is a fabrication — both a fiction and an expedient lie — and that he is at liberty to make or break connections at will: "You will want cause and effect. All right." Having laid an analogy in our path — Kekulé dreams the benzene ring in the form of the Great Serpent — he will then belabor its point to make sure we don't miss it — *"Just like that snake with its tail in its mouth*, GET IT?" — which of course robs the point of its power and ruins any confidence we might otherwise have had in the analogy.

The narrative voice in *Gravity's Rainbow* uses the conventions of novelistic realism, but he refuses the implications of those conventions. The point of the refusal is to provide rhetorical assurance that the important thing — the meaning or the subject — is never present in the narration or correlated with it by some lucid nexus of signification, but always evasive and absent. Not remotely present, but absent: not there, really, but threatening from the other side, from beyond the Zero degree of absolute writing. As Frank Kermode says, writing about the Tristero of *The Crying of Lot 49*, "That plot is pointed to as the object of some possible annunciation; but the power is in the pointing. . . . Its [the novel's] separation from its exterior and its totality are precisely what it is *about*."

Tyrone Slothrop, who at first is barely perceivable as an entity, winds up nearly inconceivable after his talent for phallic rocket-dowsing is of no further use to Them. In a curiously inverse way his paranoia pays off in his own preterition. The final *sparagmos* is a dissolution which averts destruction. Not meaningfully terminated, neither saved nor damned, he is dropped piecemeal from his own story and parsed into a scattering of ambiguous traces—a face on the cover of a record album, an undershirt stained with the blood of John Dillinger, a name here and there from which no identity may be salvaged.

Slothrop's disappearance is mirrored in the notorious paranoia of the entity (if there is one) called Thomas Pynchon. Whatever its basis in his personality (whatever and wherever that may be), Pynchon's paranoia is in the service of an authorial preterition. By refusing to permit interviews or photographs, by stubbornly remaining invisible, incognito, and incommunicado, Pynchon escapes into and through his texts. Mba-kayere. He is nothing but the signifier of occasional rumors in *Newsweek, Playboy,* and other literary journals. The paranoia and the preterition are part of the oeuvre.

Tyrone Slothrop and Thomas Pynchon follow their common father William down the way not taken, the way of the preterite. And both are lost. They are the America we did not choose. According to Mondaugen's Law, "Personal density is directly proportional to temporal bandwidth." Without past or future, Slothrop and Pynchon alike, deprived of a local habitation, scarcely left with a name, thin out to airy nothing. The America that was chosen—the American that burned William Slothrop-Pynchon's heretical book, the America that sent Tyrone Slothrop (and his time) into the Zone and into the void—also fabricated (perhaps) the paranoia of Tom Pynchon. And his book. It may even be the case—this would be the ultimate paranoid fantasy—that the two ways, of election and of preterition, are the same. The destruction willed by election and the dissolution remaindered for preterition—Gottfried the sacrifice and Slothrop the scapegoat—are at last reconciled in the nonbeing that lies over the last Δt and beyond the Zero.

00000

Cultural optimism aside, these remarks converge toward a conjecture about the rhetoric of *Gravity's Rainbow.* By rhetoric I understand, most generally and most fundamentally, the technique of linguistic recovery. Traditionally rhetoric is the persuasive use of language. Burke identifies courtship as the paradigmatic act of persuasion and regards prayer as the pure form of persuasion. The use of language to persuade posits a hierarchic distance between persuader and persuadee and at the same time, by the same use of language, wills to reduce this distance to the absolute proximity of union. Rhetoric, which acknowledges the differences among men and proposes to overcome them, attempts by means of language to achieve what Burke calls a consubstantiality of motives. Thus the lover courting his beloved linguistically abases himself and exalts her, but to the end of achieving union with her: not only a congress of the flesh, but also a communion of wills and minds and affections. Thus also prayer, in which God as the Perfect Persuadee is infinitely exalted and the worshiper as the ideal persuader infinitely abased—to the end that they may eventually be joined in a sacramental communion or mystical rapture—is the essence of persuasion.

Perhaps prayer is the *pure* form of the rhetorical act because God and the devotee are, rather obviously, linguistic entities. Unlike lover and beloved, each of whom retains an individuality and a substantiality that exceeds the bounds of their courtship, God and the worshiper are nothing but the termini of a perfectly ideal and all-encompassing relationship. At least the radical of every rhetorical situation is the relationship of language and reality. The purpose of language is to manifest being: to express, represent, comprehend. And yet the reality of the linguistic sign is an alienation of the being it wants to reveal. A hierarchy: language as sign is bound to the service of truth and reality, and a distance: the sign invariably others what it would grasp. Rhetoric, radically considered, is the endeavor, by means of language, to recover in and for language the being of which language itself is the alienation. Otherwise: rhetoric is the project of the redemption of language by the recuperation of being.

By preterition, rhetorically taken, I understand: negative recuperation. *Praeteritio,* the figure of conspicuous omission, magnified to the point of method, is a way of engaging a fundamental problem of language. Language, we have learned, cannot deliver the presence of being, a word which (following Nabokov) should therefore never be written except in scare-quotes. Reality is always distanced and deferred by the sign, and the signified by being written is always drawn into the net of signifiers. Writing is, originally and essentially, absence, and the rhetorical project is doomed. But by making the absence of being conspicuous, by weaving a text of signifiers that is excessively, loquaciously, and spectacularly vacuous, one makes the absence portentous. Portentous of that which cannot be said and must be said.

Preterite rhetoric recuperates being by not signifying it. The nonsignification does not permit the nonsignified to become a signifer; does not draw it into the web of signification, but leaves it in its alterity. Neither spider nor fly, it is glimpsed through the interstices of the web as that which is not caught. Being is recuperated only if it escapes signification, and language is redeemed only if it retains its freedom from every predestined meaning. That is the double truth of preterition and the mercy of Iscariot.

Whereof one cannot speak one must keep silent. But this silence, too, must be spoken. If they can get you asking the wrong questions, they don't have to worry about answers.

Conventional literary forms—comic, tragic, or what not—present, in the foreground or provisionally, a world broken and disordered. But in the background, and finally, stands an overriding order and unity that redeems the chaos of the interim. A background that is either written in the text or unambiguously implied by it. But in the world of the paranoid, unity and order—in their Calvinist form, the eternal decrees of God—may only be perceived as an awful absence. And only portrayed as the shadow of a possible Other falling across the mortal scene. The world that is not delivered by preterition is therefore neither tragic nor comic, neither the setting for a romantic quest nor the occasion of an ironic put-down. Preterition is a way of inscribing without foreclosing an undecidable dialectic.

One characteristic and pervasive feature of Pynchon's style, not fully explicable as a piece of 1940s slang, is his use of the demonstrative "that" where one would expect the definite article or nothing at all. The text insistently *points,* to "that" Slothrop, "that" Peenemünde, "that" *Schwarzgerät.* Ostentatiously ostensive, it draws us into itself (centripetally) by directing us away from itself (the centrifugal "that") toward a signified that is not there.

Quite. On his way to rescue Der Springer from the Russians, Slothrop, growing ever more absentminded, begins to lose his grip on the situation and the point of his presence in it:

> But just over the embankment, down in the arena, what might that have been just now, waiting in this broken moonlight, camouflage paint from fins to point crazed into jigsaw . . . is it, then, really never to find you again? Not even in your worst times of night, *with pencil words on your page only* Δt *from the things they stand for?* And inside the victim is twitching, fingering beads, touching wood, *avoiding any Operational Word.* Will it really never come to take you, now? (my emphasis)

The text / Pynchon here addresses it / himself. The absence of the signified is infinitesimal and absolute. The words on the page are only Δt away from the things they stand for. But the thing itself will (maybe) never find you, never come to take you. There is no Operational Word, only vain gestures of signification—twitching—and ineffectual conjurations of significance—fingering beads and touching wood. Nothing is created and nothing is revealed.

Language is the approach to Zero. Reality—the Rocket for which language is the predestined quest—lies always on the other side, a camouflaged apparition. *Gravity's Rainbow* exists *at*—not *in*—the interface of signifier and signified. And the "last unmeasurable gap . . . , the last delta-t" is signification, by which we are inexorably directed toward being and irreparably sundered from it.

When Captain Blicero's African *Lustknabe* uses the words *Ndjambi Karunga* (Herero for "God") to mean "fuck," the passions of the Christian pervert are inflamed. Although "to the boy Ndjambi Karunga is what happens when they couple, that's all," Blicero "feels the potency of every word: words are only an eye-twitch from the things they stand for. The peril of buggering the boy under the resonance of the sacred Name fills him insanely with lust, lust in the face—in the mask—of instant talion." It is that "eye-twitch" that makes the difference between "face" and "mask" . . . that makes all the differences. And all the difference.

Writing all by itself is a preterite act. Igor Blobadjian, party representative assigned to the G Committee of the Central Committee on the New Turkic Alphabet, observes that when an oral language is alphabetized and reduced to script, "print just goes running on without him." The inscription of the signifier is the omission of the signified. As preterition, language is innately paranoid. Like every paranoid, it suspects the sacred everywhere. Paranoia, which is "nothing less than the onset, the leading edge, of the discovery that *everything is connected,* everything in the Creation, a secondary illumination—not yet blindingly One, but at least connected, and perhaps a route In," takes linguistic form in the "mania for name-giving, dividing the Creation finer and finer, analyzing, setting namer more hopelessly apart from named."

But the alienation of the named does not eliminate the Other; on the contrary, it establishes its Otherness. Miklos Thanatz discovers that a "screen of words between himself and the numinous was always just a tactic . . . it never let him feel any freer." And Enzian (Blicero's catamite grown up) knows that although there "may be no gods . . . , there is a pattern: names by themselves may have no magic, but the *act* of naming, the physical utterance, obeys the pattern."

The paradox of language, that it can only acknowledge being by not representing it, unites the preterite's negative freedom from the constraints of destiny and the paranoid's negative presentiment of the divine transcendence. Being, its integrity unviolated by a language of appropriation and possession (conventional rhetoric), is *revealed in* preterite rhetoric just insofar as it is not *claimed for* language. At the same time and by the same strategy language retains its liberty; the signifiers, not directed toward an always already foreclosed rhetorical consummation, are allowed to go their way.

That paradox is the source of the gravity of *Gravity's Rainbow:* the overpowering weight of reality it sustains not in spite of but precisely because of the "mindless" irresponsibility of the discourse itself. In the rhetoric of Pynchon's narrative preterition is the paranoid way of showing the natures of things by not capturing them in language. Its efficacy resides, paradoxically, not in its formal perfection and self-sufficiency, but in its cultivated ineptitude and formal disarray, by which the absence of the signified is made obvious and momentous. Like Roger Mexico pissing on the System, or Franz Pökler giving his wedding ring to a bare survivor of Camp Dora, the preterition itself—the dance of signifiers that performs this monstrosity—is an act of the invisible Counterforce, the We-system that sabotages the They-system by unreason and outrage. That is, by acts of grace.

The text of *Gravity's Rainbow,* as the end approaches and the Counterforce begins its work of destruction, becomes increasingly random and disconnected. Without the presence of the transcendental signified to hold it together, the fiction dismembers and disperses itself just as it does Slothrop. In so doing it at once allows Them their alterity and absence, and preserves for Us our freedom from the determinism and bondage Their presence would entail. The exorcism of Pointsmanian, Pavlovian, Calvinist—what's in a name?—predestinations, preterition is, as *Gravity's Rainbow* itself says, "creative paranoia."

The end of the Elect and of the Reprobate is predetermined and sure. They have no option but to work out the terms (both words and conditions) of their respective destinies. Only the preterite, released from predestination by divine neglect, can play. A preterite "God," his own freedom (that is, transcendence) assured by his indifference to his handiwork, releases his creatures from the shackles of his concern and thereby guarantees *their* freedom.

An admonition, perhaps, for Pynchon's reader. Paranoia, "the normal hermeneutic activity in disease," is the appropriate motive with which to approach *Gravity's Rainbow.* Its plot, incredible and unintelligible as *mimesis praxeos,* is also imperfect as conspiracy. The authorial deity, both person and persona, having perpetrated his text and littered it with ambiguous tokens of his intention, ironically withdraws and throws the question to the reader. Is there a plan? Does it mean anything? "Consider honestly . . . which side you would rather be on." The author's preterition of his readers, his refusal to predestine their response, is the seal of their liberty; their consequent paranoia is the condition of the possibility of a creative exegesis. The innocence of the creatures is in inverse proportion to the immorality of the Master.

The Rocket of the Apocalypse fails to achieve transcendence, just as Pynchon's novel fails to deliver being or "whatever it is the word is there, buffering, to protect us from." The Rocket, both the text and its obsession, is at once the seeking and the sought. As the hope of escape from sign to significance, the Rocket is sought, ineffectually at last, by the text, which in turn is the object, elusive as it turns out, of its reader's quest. There is no escape from the circuit of signification. *You* hide, they seek.

That is why Gravity's curve — the parabola described by the Rocket that sets out to invade and conquer the alterity of heaven but halts, pauses, and plummets to earth — is a rainbow: a sign of hope. As the *Fünffachnullpunkt,* bearing the sacrifice of the peace of God, is fired, the narrator says, "This ascent will be betrayed to Gravity. . . . The victim, in bondage to falling, rises on a promise, a prophecy, of Escape."

At the other end of its flight, as the Rocket is poised on its final infinitesimal over the roof of the Orpheus Theatre in Los Angeles, at the end of the West, the screen goes dark and we ("old fans who've always been at the movies") are invited to touch the person next to us or to reach between our own cold legs, and requested to sing a hymn by William Slothrop ("Follow the bouncing ball . . ."), a song "*They* never taught anyone to sing," for "centuries forgotten and out of print" (where did it come from?). A hymn that ends with the words (reminiscent of Lake District tunesmith William Wordsworth):

> With a face on ev'ry mountainside,
> And a soul in ev'ry stone.

After these words — which may predict a state of total and final entropy or prophesy the eventual renewal of the world — there is nothing but the equally ambivalent solicitation: "Now everybody — "

00000

Gravity's Rainbow begins — almost — with the words: "It is too late." It ends — not quite — with the words: "there is time." In the inconceivable warp of language that separates these two impossible moments of time, the fiction undoes itself.

Gravity's Rainbow: An Experience in Modern Reading

Tony Tanner

Gravity's Rainbow (1973) is a novel of such vastness and range that it defies—with a determination unusual even in this age of "difficult" books—any summary. It defies quite a lot of other things as well. There are over 400 characters—we should perhaps say "names," since the ontological status of the figures that drift and stream across the pages is radically uncertain. There are many discernible, or half-discernible, plots, involving, for example, the GI Tyrone Slothrop, whose sexual encounters in London during the war uncannily anticipate where the V2 rockets fall; a rocket genius named Captain Blicero (later Major Weissmann); Franz Pökler, who worked on the rocket but is hoping to retrieve his wife and daughter from the concentration camps; Tchitcherine, a Soviet intelligence officer (who, among other things, has to impose a Latin alphabet on an illiterate tribe in central Asia); Enzian, his half-brother and leader of the *Schwarzkommando*, a Herero group exiled in Germany from South-West Africa which is trying to assemble the secrets of the rocket, and which also seems bent on self-annihilation. These plots touch and intersect, or diverge and separate, as the case may be. Somewhere at the back of them all is the discovery by the nineteenth-century German chemist, Kekulé von Stradonitz, of the model of the benzene ring, which made possible the manufacture of the molecular structures of plastic and, ultimately, rocketry.

There is a good deal of well-informed technological reference in the book—

From *Thomas Pynchon.* © 1982 by Tony Tanner. Methuen, 1982. Originally entitled *"Gravity's Rainbow."*

inserted not gratuitously but to demonstrate how technology has created its own kind of people (servants) with their own kind of consciousness (or lack of it). There is evidence of a whole range of knowledge of contemporary "specialized" expertises—from mathematics, chemistry and ballistics, to classical music theory, film and comic strips. There is also a prevailing sense of the degree to which modern life has been bureaucratized and turned into an impersonal routine (Max Weber is alluded to and his phrase "the routinization of charisma" quoted twice —as Edward Mendelson, again, was the first to point out). As before, many other writers are alluded to, directly or indirectly—Melville, Conrad, Faulkner, Emily Dickinson, Whitman, Rilke (crucial), Borges (always important for Pynchon, but in this novel finally named), etc. Out of all this—and much, much more—Pynchon has created a book that is both one of the great historical novels of our time and arguably the most important literary text since *Ulysses*.

I think it is important to stress that the novel provides an exemplary experience in modern reading. The reader does not move comfortably from some ideal "emptiness" of meaning to a satisfying fullness but instead becomes involved in a process in which any perception can precipitate a new confusion, and an apparent clarification turn into a prelude to further difficulties. So far from this being an obstacle to appreciating the book, it is part of its essence. It is the way we live now.

Gravity's Rainbow does indeed have a recognizable historical setting. It is engaged with Europe at the end of the Second World War and just after. In choosing to situate his novel at this point in time, Pynchon is concentrating on a crucial moment when a new transpolitical order began to emerge out of the ruins of old orders that could no longer maintain themselves. At one point he describes the movements of displaced people at the end of the war, "a great frontierless streaming." The sentences that follow mime out this "frontierless" condition in an extraordinary flow of objects and people, and conclude: "so the populations move, across the open meadow, limping, marching, shuffling, carried, hauling along the detritus of an order, a European and bourgeois order they don't yet know is destroyed forever." A later passage suggests what is taking the place of this vanished order. "Oh, a State begins to take form in the stateless German night, a State that spans oceans and surface politics, sovereign as the International or the Church of Rome, and the Rocket is its soul."

The Rocket is specifically the V2, which was launched on London and, because it travelled faster than sound, crashed before the sound of its flight could be heard—a frightening disruption of conventional sequence and cause-effect expectations. (Hence the famous opening sentence, "a screaming comes across the sky.") It also becomes the paradigm product of modern technology, and in making it the central object of the book, Pynchon is clearly addressing himself to the sociopolitical implications of contemporary trends in history. But he refuses to do this in a conventional narrative way because conventional narrative procedures were themselves products of that vanished bourgeois order, and it is no longer possible to "read" what is going on in any conventional manner. Thus Pynchon's characters move in a world of both too many and too few signs, too much data and too little information, too many texts but no reliable editions, an extreme "overabundance of signifer," to borrow a phrase from Lévi-Strauss. I stress this first because, before attempting to indicate what the novel is "about" in any traditional sense, I think it is important to consider how to read it, for more than anything else this book provides an experience in modern reading. People who expect and demand the traditional narrative conventions will be immediately disoriented by this book.

There is one phantasmagoric episode in a "disquieting structure" which is a dream-version of some contemporary hell. We read: "It seems to be some very extensive museum, a place of many levels, and new wings that generate like living tissue—though if it all does grow toward some end shape, those who are here inside can't see it." Now not only is this applicable to all the dozens of characters in the book itself—drifting in and out of sections, participating in different spaces, finding themselves on different levels; it is both their *dream* and their *dread* to see an "end shape" to it all, though of course, being in the book, they never will. But—and I think this is very important—nor do we as readers. One of the things Pynchon manages to do so brilliantly is to make us participate in the beset and bewildered consciousness which is the unavoidable affliction of his characters.

As you read the book you seem to pass through a bewildering variety of genres, behavioural modes, and types of discourse: at different times the text seems to partake of such different things as pantomime, burlesque, cinema, cabaret, card games, songs, comic strips, spy stories, serious history, encyclopedic information, mystical and visionary meditations, the scrambled imagery of dreams, the cold cause-and-effect talk of the behaviourists, and all the various ways in which men try to control and coerce realities both seen and unseen— from magic to measurement, from science to seances. At one point, one character is reading a Plasticman comic; he is approached by a man of encyclopedic erudition, who engages him in a conversation about etymology. Here is a clue for us: we should imagine that we are reading a comic, but it is partly transparent, and through it we are also reading an encyclopedia, a film script, a piece of science history, and so on. There is only one text but it contains a multiplicity of surfaces; modes of discourse are constantly turning into objects of discourse with no one stable discourse holding them together.

This is not such a bizarre undertaking as it may sound. We can all read and decode the different languages and genres Pynchon has brought into his book.

Modern man is above all an interpreter of different signs, a reader of differing discourses, a servant of signals, a compelled and often compulsive decipherer. In Henri Lefebvre's use of the word, we do live in a "pleonastic" society of "aimless signifiers and disconnected signifieds" on many levels, so that you can see evidence of hyperredundancy in the realm of signs, objects, institutions, even human beings. Wherever we look, there is too much to "read" ("Is it any wonder the world's gone insane, with information come to be the only real medium of exchange?"). But never before has there been such uncertainty about the reliability of the texts. One character in the novel, making his way across the wastelands of postwar Europe, wonders whether it does contain a "Real Text." He thinks that such a text may be connected with the secrets of the rocket; but perhaps the "Real Text" is the desolate landscape he is traversing, or perhaps he missed the Real Text somewhere behind him in a ruined city . . . . Reading Pynchon's novel gives us a renewed sense of how we have to read the modern world. At times in his book it is not always clear whether we are in a bombed-out building or a bombed-out mind, but that, too, is quite appropriate. For how many of those rockets that fell in London fell in the consciousness of the survivors, exploding in the modern mind? And, looking around and inside us, how can we be sure how much is Real Text, and how much is ruined debris?

In all this it is impossible to say with confidence what the book is "about," but constantly you have the sense of many things that it seems to be about. We might consider the title, or titles, of the novel. Originally it was to be called *Mindless Pleasures.* We can perhaps infer the intention behind such a title from a passage in which a girl, Jessica, temporarily in love with the rebellious Roger Mexico (of whom more later), thinks of her other suitor, Jeremy, who is the quintessence of the Establishment.

> Jeremy *is* the War, he is every assertion the fucking War has ever made — that we are meant for work and government, for austerity: and these shall take priority over love, dreams, the spirit, the senses and the other second-class trivia that are found among the idle and mindless hours of the day. . . . Damn them, they are wrong.

Pynchon has ever been a sympathetic supporter of "second-class trivia," which would seem to include those "mindless" pleasures that have no interest in "the War," which "the War" — and all the official organization, technology and bureaucracy it represents (is the product of) — dismisses and disavows. One basic struggle or opposition in the book, then, is indeed between "mindless pleasures" and the all-too-mindful pains and perversions of "the War."

The second title suggests the opposition another way. The "Rainbow" inevitably triggers reminiscences of the rainbow in Genesis, which was God's covenant to Noah "and every living creature of all flesh that *is* upon the earth" that there would be no more destruction on the earth. Gravity, by contrast, is that law (not a "covenant") by which all things — "and all flesh that *is* upon the earth" — are finally, inexorably, drawn back down and into the earth: an absolutely neutral promise that all living things will die. The trajectory of the rocket — which at the end of the novel is both a womb (it contains the living figure of Gottfried) and a coffin (arguably embodying the death and perversion of all life-giving love and sexuality) — exactly enacts this stark ironic ambiguity. And in this apparent hopelessly proliferating novel the rocket is always there. It is phallic and fatal, Eros transformed into Thanatos, invading "Gravity's grey eminence" only to succumb to it, curving through the sky like a lethal rainbow, then crashing to the earth. Does it strike by "chance" or according to some hidden design, some "music" of annihilation which we shall never hear but which is always being played?

Around the rocket and its production Pynchon builds up a version of war-time England and postwar Europe which is staggering in both its detail and its fantasy. In addition, the novel, as if trying to reach out into wider and more comprehensive contexts, extends back into colonial and American history, down into the world of molecules, up into the stars, back even to Bethlehem when men saw another kind of burning light in the sky. In all this, certain abiding preoccupations may be discerned. Pattern, plots and paranoia — these are familiar in Pynchon's world; add to those paper, plastic, preterition, probability theory and Pavlovian conditioning, and some of the main themes have been listed. (The alliteration is not, of course, accidental: Pynchon, as author, knows that he is engaged in an activity related to Stencil's search for V. Unlike Stencil, however, he is constantly breaking up the gathering pattern of echoes, clues and similarities.)

What emerges from the book is a sense of a force and a system — something, someone, referred to simply as "the firm" or "They" — which is actively trying to bring everything to zero and beyond, trying to institute a world of nonbeing, an operative kingdom of death, covering the organic world with a world of paper and plastic and transforming all natural resources into destructive power and waste: the rocket and the debris around it. "They" are precisely nonspecific, unlocatable. There is always the possibility of a They behind the They, a plot behind the plot; the quest to identify "Them" sucks the would-be identifier into the possibility of an endless regression. But, whatever Their source and origin, They are dedicated to annihilation. This is a vision of entropy as an extremely powerful worldwide, if not cosmos-wide, enterprise. From Their point of view, and in the world of insidious reversals and inversions They are instituting, the war was a great creative act, not the destruction but the "reconfiguration" of people and places. They are also identified with "the System" which removes

> from the rest of the World these vast quantities of energy to keep its own tiny desperate fraction showing a profit. . . . The System may or may not understand that it's only buying time . . . [that it] sooner or later must crash to its death, when its addiction to energy has become more than the rest of the World can supply. . . . Living inside the System is like riding across the country in a bus driven by a maniac bent on suicide.

The ecological relevance of this is all too frighteningly obvious.

Inside the System everything is fixed and patterned, but its organizing cen-tre — its "soul" — is the rocket. To the extent that the System and everyone inside the System in one way or another converge on the rocket, they are converging on death. Outside the System, and one of its by-products as it were, is the Zone in which nothing is fixed and there are no patterns or points of convergence. There are "no zones but the Zone" says one voice. This is the area of "the new Uncer-tainty": "in the Zone categories have been blurred badly." In the Zone every-thing and everyone is adrift, for there are no taxonomies, and no narratives, to arrange them. If all the concepts are blurred, can the people in the Zone have any knowledge of reality, or are they perhaps nearer to reality by living in a decon-ceptualized state, fumbling around among the debris left when the prisonhouse of language itself seems to have been destroyed? In the Zone there are only "im-ages of Uncertainty." This involves a release from feeling that one is living in a completely patterned and determinate world, but also a panic at being outside any containing and explaining "frame" (in his review Richard Poirier wrote at length on the significance of the "frame" throughout the book). Those outside the System seem doomed to go on "kicking endlessly among the plastic trivia, finding in each Deeper Significance, and trying to string them all together . . . to bring them together, in their slick persistence and our preterition . . . to make sense out of, to find the meanest sharp sliver of truth in so much replica-tion, so much waste."

Figures in the book inhabit either the System or the Zone or move between them (or do not know whether they are in either or both, for of course System and Zone have no locational as well as no epistemological stability), and this in turn elicits two dominant states of mind: paranoia and anti-paranoia. Paranoia is, in terms of the book, "nothing less than the onset, the leading edge, of the dis-covery that *everything is connected,* everything in the Creation, a secondary illumi-nation — not yet blindingly One, but at least connected." Of course, everything depends on the nature of the connection, the intention revealed in the pattern; and just *what* it is that may connect everything in Pynchon's world is what wor-ries his main characters, like Slothrop. Paranoia is also related to the Puritan obsession with seeing signs in everything, particularly signs of an angry God. Pynchon makes the connection clear by referring to "a Puritan reflex of seeking other orders behind the visible, also known as paranoia." The opposite state of mind is anti-paranoia, "where nothing is connected to anything, a condition not many of us can bear for long." (This may be a reference to the lines in *The Waste Land:*

> On Margate Sands.
> I can connect
> Nothing with nothing.
> ("The Fire Sermon")

And, as figures move between System and Zone, so they oscillate between paranoia and anti-paranoia, shifting from a seething blank of unmeaning to the sinister apparent legibility of an unconsoling labyrinthine pattern or plot. "We are obsessed with building labyrinths, where before there was open plain and sky. To draw ever more complex patterns on the blank sheet. We cannot abide that *openness;* it is terror to us." Those who do not accept the officially sanctioned "delusions" of the System as "truth," but cannot abide pure blankness, have to seek out other modes of interpretation. Thus "Those like Slothrop, with the greatest interest in discovering the truth, were thrown back on dreams, psychic flashes, omens, cryptographies, drug-epistemologies, all dancing on a ground of terror, contradiction, absurdity." This is the carnival of modern consciousness which the book itself portrays.

All this is related to our situation as readers. To put it very crudely, the book dramatizes two related assemblings and disassemblings — of the rocket, and of the character or figure named Slothrop. Slothrop is engaged in trying to find out the secret of how the rocket is assembled, but in the process he himself is disassembled. Similarly the book both assembles and disassembles itself as we try to read it. For, just as many of the characters are trying to see whether there is a "text" within the "waste" and a "game behind the game," that is what we are having to do with the book as it unfolds in our attention. There is deliberately too much evidence, partaking of too many orders of types of explanation and modes of experience for us to hold it all together. Reading itself thus becomes a paranoid activity which is, however, constantly breaking down under the feeling that we shall never arrive at a unitary reading, never hold the book in one "frame": the sense of indeterminateness is constantly encroaching on us. We fluctuate between System and Zone, paranoia and anti-paranoia, experiencing both the dread of reducing everything to one fixed explanation — an all-embracing plot of death — and the danger of succumbing to apparently random detritus.

Behind all this is the process of nature itself, working by organization and disorganization. The rocket is described as "an entire system *won,* away from the feminine darkness, held against the entropies of lovable but scatterbrained Mother Nature." It engorges energy and information in its "fearful assembly"; thus its "order" is obtained at the cost of an increase in disorder in the world around it, through which so many of the characters stumble. But in its fixity and metallic destructive inhumanity it is an order of death — a *negative* parallel of the process of nature, since its disintegration presages no consequent renewal and growth. That is one reason why at the end the rocket is envisaged as *containing* the living body of a young man (Gottfried), for this is the System *inside* which man is plotting his own annihilation. If we as readers try to win away one narrative "system" from the book, we are in danger of repeating mentally what They are doing in building the rocket. To put it in its most extreme form, They are trying to reduce all of nature's self-renewing variety to one terminal rocket; we must avoid the temptation to reduce the book to one fixed meaning. That is why our reading should be paranoid and anti-paranoid, registering narrative order and disorder, experiencing both the determinate and the indeterminate, pattern and randomness, renewing our awareness of our acts and interpretations as being both conditioned and free, and of ourselves as synthesizing and disintegrating systems.

In this way we can to some extent be released from the System-Zone bind which besets Pynchon's main characters, in particular the figure of Slothrop. What happens to Slothrop is in every sense exemplary. One of the earliest events in his life is being experimented on in a Pavlovian laboratory (which is related to the obsession with all kinds of control and "conditioning" that the book also explores). He is last seen, if seen at all, on a record cover. In between he has been the Plasticman and Rocketman of the comics he reads, played a variety of roles for English and American intelligence, been involved in the distorted fantasies and plots of dozens of figures in postwar Europe, all the time approaching the centre, the secret of the rocket, which is also the absolute zero at the heart of the System. He knows that he is involved in the evil games of other people, whether they are run by the army or black marketeers or whatever, but he cannot finally get out of these games. Indeed, leaving all the games is one of the hopes and dreams of the few people with any human feeling left in the book. But it remains a dream. (This is problematical. Of one character we read: "Pökler committed then his act of courage. He quit the game." And an earlier comment seems to allow of this possibility:

> But now and then, players in a game will, lull or crisis, be reminded
> how it is, after all, really play — and be unable then to continue in the
> same spirit. . . . Nor need it be anything sudden, spectacular — it
> may come in gentle — and regardless of the score, the number of

watchers, their collective wish, penalties they or the Leagues may impose, the player will, waking deliberately . . . say *fuck it* and quit the game, quit it cold.

The problem is that there seems to be nowhere to go if you "quit the game"—though I suppose it could be an internal secession—unless it means to get lost in the Zone. But that is not an unequivocal experience.)

Reality has been preempted by games, or it has been replaced by films, so that people can be said to live "paracinematic lives." As Slothrop moves through different experience-spaces, he suffers a loss of emotion, a "numbness," and a growing sense that he will never "get back." Along with this erosion of the capacity to feel, he begins to "scatter," his "sense of Now" or "temporal band-width" gets narrower and narrower, and there is a feeling that he is getting so lost and unconnected that he is vaporizing out of time and place altogether. Near the end of his travels, Slothrop suddenly sees a rainbow, a real one, and he has a vision of its entering into sexual union with the green unpapered earth; it is the life-giving antithesis to the rocket's annihilating penetrations: "and he stands crying, not a thing in his head, just feeling natural." After that he effectively vanishes. There is a story told about him.

> [He] was sent into the Zone to be present at his own assembly—perhaps, heavily paranoid voices have whispered, *his time's assembly*—and there ought to be a punch line to it, but there isn't. The plan went wrong. He is being broken down instead, and scattered.

The disassembling of Slothrop is, as I have suggested, in some way related to the assembling of the rocket—the plan that went *right*—and it has far-reaching and disturbing implications.

The last comment on the possible whereabouts of Slothrop is this: "we would expect to look among the Humility, among the gray and preterite souls, to look for him adrift in the hostile light of the sky, the darkness of the sea." This idea of "the preterite" is very important in this book and, I think, central to Pynchon's vision; as he uses it, it refers to those who have been "passed over," those he has always been interested in, the abandoned, the neglected, the despised and the rejected, those for whom the System has no use, the human junk thrown overboard from the ship of state (a literal ship in this book, incidentally, named *Anubis* after the ancient Egyptian God of the Dead). Set against the preterite are the élite, the users and manipulators, those who regard the planet as solely for their satisfaction, the nameless and ubiquitous "They" who dominate the world of the book. One of the modern malaises Pynchon has diagnosed is that it is possible for a person to feel himself entering into a state of "preterition." But—and once again Pynchon's erudition and wit work admirably here—the idea of humanity being divided into a preterite and an élite or elect is of course a basic Puritan belief. In theological terms, the preterite were precisely those who were not elected by God and, if I may quote from one of those chilling Puritan pronouncements, "the preterite are damned because they were never meant to be saved." In redeploying these terms, which after all were central to the thinking of the people who founded America, and applying them to cruelly divisive and oppositional modes of thought at work throughout the world today, Pynchon once again shows how imaginatively he can bring the past and present together.

One of Slothrop's ancestors wrote a book called *On Preterition,* supporting the preterite as being quite as important as the elect, and Slothrop himself wonders whether this doesn't point to a fork in the road which America never took, and whether there might not be a "way back" even in the ruined spaces of postwar Europe:

> maybe for a little while all the fences are down, one road as good as another, the whole space of the Zone cleared, depolarized, and somewhere inside the waste of it a single set of coordinates from which to proceed, without elect, without preterite, without even nationality to fuck it up.

This, then, is the organizing question of the book. Is there a way back? (Page 1 signals this question: "Is this the way out?") Out of the streets "now indifferently gray with commerce"; out of the City of Pain, which Pynchon has taken over from Rilke's Tenth Duino Elegy and offers as a reflection of the world we have made; a way back out of the cinemas, the laboratories, the asylums and all our architecture of mental drugging, coercion and disarray (derangement)? Out of a world in which emotions have been transferred from people to things, and where images supplant realities? Where, ultimately, would the "way back" lead, if not to some lost Eden previous to all categories and taxonomies, election and preterition, divisions and oppositions? Can we even struggle to regain such a mythic state? Of course the book offers no answers, though the possibility of a "counterforce" is touched on.

The last section of the novel is indeed entitled "The Counterforce," and one figure, Tchitcherine, is convinced "There is a counterforce in the Zone." But if there is an active "counterforce" it would seem to be vitiated by its contact with, and contamination by, the System. A crucial figure in this possible counterforce is Roger Mexico, and there are some of his late doubts about its viability or possible effectiveness.

> Well, if the Counterforce knew better what those categories concealed, they might be in a better position to disarm, de-penis and

and dismantle the Man. But they don't. Actually they do, but they don't admit it. Sad but true. They are as schizoid, as double-minded in the massive presence of money, as any of the rest of us, and that's the hard fact. The Man has a branch office in each of our brains, his corporate emblem is a white albatross, each local rep has a cover known as the Ego, and their mission in this world is Bad Shit. We do know what's going on, and we let it go on . . . which is worse: living on as Their pet, or death? It is not a question he has ever imagined himself asking seriously. It has come by surprise, but there's no sending it away now, he really does have to decide, and soon enough, plausibly soon, to feel the terror in his bowels. Terror he cannot think away. He has to choose between his life and his death. Letting it sit for a while is no compromise, but a decision to live, on Their terms.

In the event, all that Roger Mexico achieves (along with Seaman Bodine, an old Pynchon figure) is the disruption of an official dinner with obscene language. It is a gesture against the binding power of the official language but not much more.

We hear no more of Roger Mexico after this incident. But, in a world dominated by the firm, the System, They, he does represent two crucial potential "counterforces"—in brief, "probability" and love. There are a number of references to probability theory in the book, and their relevance can be appreciated if we recall Oedipa Maas caught between zeroes and ones as she found herself forced into a mental prison of binary oppositions at the end of *Lot 49*. In *Gravity's Rainbow* the behaviourist Pavlovian scientist Pointsman is absolutely a zero/one man, and "If ever the Antipointsman existed, Roger Mexico is the man"—because Mexico, who works with "probability," can exist and operate in those "excluded middles" that in Pynchon represent the area of unforeseen possibilities and diversities. One passage makes this clear:

> But in the domain of zero to one, not-something to something, Pointsman can only possess the zero and the one. He cannot, like Mexico, survive anyplace in between. . . . But to Mexico belongs the domain *between* zero and one—the middle Pointsman has excluded from his persuasion—the probabilities.

It has the effect of keeping open a gap in the systematized and systematic thinking of the System. That thinking can only accept cause-and-effect thinking, because that makes possible a fantasy of total control ("*We must never lose control,*" thinks Pointsman); but Mexico can see further:

> there's a feeling about that cause-and-effect may have been taken as far as it will go. That for science to carry on at all, it must look for a

less narrow, a less . . . sterile set of assumptions. The next great breakthrough may come when we have the courage to junk cause-and-effect entirely, and strike off at some other angle.

Striking off at "some other angle" would involve recognizing and accepting "probability," "indeterminacy" and "discontinuity" in the "curve of life." All these modes of thought are enacted in the text itself (we are seldom confronted with zero / one choices; more often we find ourselves groping away in the forgotten richness — and darkness — of those excluded middles). But whether they are sufficient to *act* as a counterforce is less clear.

It might be asked if there are any other hints of effective positives — counterforces — in the book. Roger Mexico is one of the very, very few figures who experience a genuine kind of "love" (with Jessica), based on real feeling, mutuality, loss of ego, true sensuality. But their love episode is, as it were, a furtive piece of borrowed time during the war; it does not survive, and Jessica turns to the Establishment figure of Jeremy as "safer." There is indeed very little love in the book: perversion and betrayal (the children especially suffer) seem to dominate, not to mention various forms and degrees of extermination and mutilation. Religious hope is teasingly glimpsed at. During the truly astonishing passage describing the Christmas vespers attended by Roger and Jessica, with reference to the magi Pynchon writes:

> Will the child gaze up from his ground of golden straw then, gaze into the eyes of the old king who bends long and unfurling overhead, leans to proffer his gift, will the eyes meet, and what message, what possible greeting or entente will flow between the king and the infant prince? Is the baby smiling, or is it just gas? Which do you want it to be?

The text suddenly flashes a half-ironic choice at us — to leave us unsettled between miracle and technology. But it hardly suggests any coming kind of salvation or true transcendence. Indeed, most of the figures in the book are somewhat like Barnardine in *Measure for Measure* (to turn again to what is obviously an important play for Pynchon), "insensible of mortality, and desperately mortal" (IV.ii). After the Advent service Roger and Jessica long for

> another night that could actually, with love and cockcrows, light the path home, banish the Adversary, destroy the boundaries between our lands, our bodies, our stories, all false, about who we are: for the one night, leaving only the clear way home and the memory of the infant you saw.

But they find no such "clear way home" and have to look for "the path you must create by yourself, alone in the dark." And that is the situation of most of the figures in the book. There are some traces of decent human feeling: strangers occasionally help, and among the "Humility" there are still "a few small chances for mercy." Kindness is mentioned—"kindness is a sturdy enough ship for these oceans"—but is insufficiently practised. Positive, generous, good human feelings and hopes and aspirations have not entirely vanished, but they are everywhere in retreat, and the attrition rate among them is dire. The counterforce (or counterforces) may have some kind of vestigial or underground existence. But it is not to be counted on.

There are recurring dreams of "freedom"—never realized—but if there is any hope it seems to reside in "the Earth": Enzian dreams that "Somewhere, among the wastes of the World, is the key that will bring us back, restore us to our Earth and to our freedom," and in a late section headed "Streets" that hope is again inscribed: "But in each of these streets, some vestige of humanity, of Earth, has to remain. No matter what has been done to it, no matter what it's been used for."

This perhaps desperate faith in the regenerative powers of "the Earth" accounts, I think, for a rather strange episode which follows immediately after the opening scene of the book. Pirate Prentice (the first named figure in the book, and of distinct importance) holds one of his Banana Breakfasts. Up on the roof of his maisonette in London there is a heap of old earth (and dead leaves and vomit and other decaying bits of organic life)—"all got scumbled together, eventually, by the knives of the seasons, to an impasto, feet thick, of unbelievable black topsoil in which anything could grow, not the least being bananas." So, in the midst of the destruction of war, growth, willy-nilly, continues. The Banana Breakfast is a fairly chaotic, farcical affair, but the bananas themselves—an unlikely enough presence in wartime London—signal a crucial phenomenon.

> Now there grows among all the rooms . . . the fragile, musaceous odor of Breakfast: flowery, permeating, surprising, more than the color of winter sunlight, taking over not so much through any brute pungency or volume as by the high intricacy to the weaving of its molecules, sharing the conjuror's secret by which—though it is not often Death is told so clearly to fuck off—the living genetic chains prove even labyrinthine enough to preserve some human face down ten or twenty generations . . . so the same assertion-through-structure allows this war morning's banana fragrance to meander, repossess, prevail. Is there any reason not to open every window, and let the kind scent blanket all Chelsea? As a spell, against falling objects.

The banana — a comic enough "spell" to set against the rocket — is nevertheless evidence of that endless generative power of the earth, that "assertion-through-structure" which is the one real hope — perhaps the only genuine counterforce — against "Their several entropies," and that accelerating movement towards death which seems to mark so many areas of the book.

The book moves to a climax that is a sort of terminal fusion of many of the key fantasies and obsessions in the book. It takes place in the American West ("of course Empire took its way westward, what other way was there but into those virgin sunsets to penetrate and to foul?"; Pynchon's book follows), and it should be noted that the last section as a whole becomes extremely difficult — impossible — to "follow" in any way at all, as though the book demonstrates how any kind of narrative that seems to link together fragments and images is becoming impossible. The warning has been sounded earlier on: "Nobody ever said a day has to be juggled into any kind of sense at day's end" — or a book at book's end. Indeed, we are systematically juggled out of sense (any recognizable sense, at least), not allowed that repose and reassurance that any sense of completed narrative can bring. Yet the very last moment seems clear enough — and sufficiently disturbing. The opening page of the novel evokes the evacuation of London, with a crucial interposed comment: "but it's all theatre." On the very last page we are back in a theatre. We are waiting for the show to start; as Pynchon comments, we have "always been at the movies (haven't we?)." The film has broken down, though on the darkening screen there is something else — a film we have not learned to see." The audience is invited to sing, while outside the rocket "reaches its last unmeasurable gap above the roof of this old theatre." It is falling in absolute silence, and we know that it will demolish the old theatre — the old theatre of what is left of our civilization. But we don't see it because we are *in* the theatre trying to read the film behind the film; and we won't hear it because, under the new dispensation, the annihilation arrives first, and only after "a screaming comes across the sky."

To argue on behalf of Pynchon's importance as a writer would be supererogatory. Placing him in a larger context is more difficult. More difficult, because he seems aware of all the literature that preceded him as well as the writing that surrounds him. From one point of view, he emerges from that extraordinary proliferation of experimentation in the novel which so deeply shaped the direction of American fiction during the 1960s and 1970s. Thus he takes his place in a period of American writing that includes such authors as William Burroughs, Joseph Heller, John Hawkes, John Barth, Robert Coover, Rudolph Wurlitzer, Ishmael Reed, Norman Mailer, Saul Bellow, and many others. The aesthetic funds alive at this time were various, but in particular I believe he was affected by the work of William Gaddis, whose novel *The Recognitions* (1955) exerted a general influence that has yet to be fully traced. This generation of American writers was in turn influenced by many European and South-American writers—in particular, Jorge Luis Borges and Vladimir Nabokov, but also Samuel Beckett, Italo Calvino, Gabriel García Marquez, Alain Robbe-Grillet and Günter Grass. That list could be extended; but suffice it to say that Pynchon was writing his novels during an extraordinarily rich time of ferment and innovation in the contemporary novel, and quickly became one of its essential voices.

However, looked at from another angle, Pynchon's work takes its place in that line of dazzlingly daring, even idiosyncratic American writing which leads back through writers like Faulkner to Mark Twain and Hawthorne, and above all to Melville and *Moby-Dick*. And, taking yet another view, we might want to cite *Tristram Shandy* as an earlier experimental novel that lies behind him; but then Sterne points us in turn back to Rabelais, and both bear the mark of *Don Quixote* (as does Pynchon)—which is, in a manner of speaking, where the novel as we know it in the West began. Few major modern writers have not in some fashion returned to these origins, and thus we can see Pynchon continuing that series of radical shifts and innovations in fictional technique which was started by Conrad and James, and continued by Joyce—all of whom are more or less audible in his work. Which is all to say that he is both creatively eclectic and unmistakably original. From one point of view, the novel from its inception has always been a mixed genre with no certain limits or prescribed formal constraints; Pynchon, then, is in no way an "eccentric" novelist, for the novel has no determined centre. Rather he is a key contemporary figure in the great tradition of those who extend the possibilities of fiction-making in arresting and enriching ways— not in this or that "Great Tradition," but in the great tradition of the novel itself.

Recognizing Reality, Realizing Responsibility

Craig Hansen Werner

Nothing since *Finnegans Wake* cries for commitment like the first sentences of *Gravity's Rainbow:* "A screaming comes across the sky. It has happened before, but there is nothing to compare it to now." Is the screaming human or the inanimate descent of the rocket? Is the coming messianic? Sexual? Is there actually "nothing" to compare it to; are we orphans in a void? Or has nothing else ever been as important as our agony? When we read Pynchon we decide, or They have already decided for us, how we live. Pynchon, shunning the robes of the aesthetic priest, preaches for the preterite, never dogmatic, but doomed (like one of his characters) to know "how phony it looks. Who will believe that in his heart he wants to belong to them out there, the vast Humility sleepless, dying, in pain tonight across the Zone? the preterite he loves, knowing he's always to be a stranger." However it looks, *Gravity's Rainbow* belongs to and with the wretched of the earth.

The screaming's human.

If we don't believe it's important now, we never will.

And our decisions are more important than any questions of literary influence or tradition. Our decisions can take us out of our conceptual systems into a life where the issues are worth talking about, where they have something to do with our humanity. Pynchon forces the resolution of modes off the page and into our lives, where it belongs. If we let him.

From *Paradoxical Resolutions: American Fiction Since James Joyce.* © 1982 by the Board of Trustees of the University of Illinois. University of Illinois Press, 1982. Originally entitled "Recognizing Reality, Realizing Responsibility: Joyce, Gaddis, Pynchon."

Joyce did influence *Gravity's Rainbow,* but he did not dominate it or direct it. Several critics have noted parallels between *Gravity's Rainbow* and *Ulysses:* both resolve questions of literary mode by rendering them irrelevant; both extend symbolic and realistic modes until they seem meaningless impositions of abstract systems on a concrete reading experience. Joyce reinforces his stylistic resolution by portraying his characters successfully resolving their experiences. Pynchon, less sure both of his own aesthetic resolution and of the ability of any individual to effect a resolution, demands that any resolution take place in the minds and lives of his real readers—you and me—rather than in an abstract "life" on the printed page. While literature is a part of "real life," it works on us individually; Pynchon challenges us to reach beyond our solipsism and to contact our preterite brothers and sisters.

Inferring Pynchon's "position" on any issue is dangerous. We simply don't know much about him. Still, *Gravity's Rainbow* provides sufficient evidence to suggest that Pynchon reacts to Joyce ambivalently. It alludes to numerous modern novelists, including Kerouac and Henry Miller, Beckett and Proust, Ellison, [and] Gaddis. While Pynchon frequently catalogs the names of important scientists, he *names* few novelists, most notably Ishmael Reed and Joyce. The direct reference to Joyce suggests Pynchon's belief that at times Joyce, too, felt drawn to the preterite: "Lenin, Trotsky, James Joyce, Dr. Einstein all sat out at these tables. Whatever it was *they* all had in common: whatever they'd come to this vantage to score . . . perhaps it had to do with the people somehow, with pedestrian mortality, restless crisscrossing of needs or desperations in one fateful piece of street . . . dialectics, matrices, archetypes all need to connect, once in a while, back to some of that proletarian blood, to body odors and senseless screaming across a table, to cheating and last hopes, or else all is dusty Dracularity, the West's ancient curse." The small "t" in "they" which Pynchon emphasizes with italics hints that he sees Joyce in essential conflict with the capital T They who have no sense of the screaming of the preterite.

Several other allusions to Joyce in *Gravity's Rainbow,* however, emphasize Joyce's participation in the destructive elitism of western culture. Identifying 1904, the year of *Ulysses'* action, as one of the "critical points" of history when some major change might have been possible, Pynchon quickly asserts that, in fact, nothing changed: "1904, Achtfaden. Ha, ha! *That's* a better joke on you than any singed asshole, all right. Lotta good it does *you.* You can't swim upstream, not under the present dispensation anyhow, all you can do is attach the number to it and suffer." At times Pynchon openly rejects the entire Joycean dedication to craft, the dedication which drew Joyce to the mythic figure of Daedalus: "Weissmann's cruelty was no less resourceful than Pökler's own engineering skill, the gift of Daedalus that allowed him to put as much labyrinth as required between himself and the inconvenience of caring." If Pynchon feels an affinity with Joyce, he qualifies it so as to preclude any temptation to compress *Gravity's Rainbow* into a narrowly Joycean mold. One of the ironies of the reception of *Gravity's Rainbow* has been the development of an image of the book as a new *Finnegans Wake*, inaccessible to all but a highly educated elite. The *Wake* indeed presents the reader with numerous puzzles, some demanding special knowledge for solution. Doomed by his vision of complexity, Pynchon uses a vocabulary no more complex than his content absolutely demands and employs numerous popular cultural references in a way which emphasizes his desire to communicate with the very people who are least likely to read his book. Joyce wanted to be studied as well as read; Pynchon would clearly accept the reading.

Pynchon's "attacks" on Joyce reflect his distrust of attempts to include reality within systems: scientific, literary, religious, whatever. To Pynchon, attempts to impose systematic constraints on experience are murderous: Pointsman (following Pavlov) struggles to explain all life in behaviorist terms because he feels threatened by the idea that another shares his own complexity. Pointsman's meditation on Pavlov reveals that he values his system more highly than human life:

> Pavlov thought that all the diseases of the mind could be explained, eventually, by the ultraparadoxical phase, the pathologically inert points on the cortex, the confusion of the ideas of the opposite. He died at the very threshold of putting these things on an experimental basis. But I live. I have the funding, and the time, and the will. Slothrop is a strong imperturbable. It won't be easy to send him into any of the three phases. We may finally have to starve, terrorize.

Weissmann's analogous vision of humanity as simple raw material for propagating his own obsessions inspires some of Pynchon's most bitter prose.

> What more do they want? She asks this seriously, as if there's a real conversion factor between information and lives. Well, strange to say, there is. Written down in the Manual, on file at the War Department. Don't forget the real business of the War is buying and selling. The murdering and the violence are self-policing, and can be entrusted to non-professionals. The mass nature of wartime death is useful in many ways. It serves as a spectacle, as diversion from the real movements of the War. It provides raw material to be recorded into History, so that children may be taught History as sequences of violence, battle after battle, and be more prepared for the adult world. Best of all, mass death's a stimulus to just ordinary folks, little fellows, to try 'n' grab a piece of that Pie while they're still here to gobble it up. The true war is a celebration of markets.

The Daedalus figure (the film director Gerhardt von Göll — der Springer) provides the artistic analog to the scientific and economic systemizer. Von Göll believes that the people he meets are literally his creations: "His film has somehow brought them into being. 'It is my mission,' he announces to Squalidozzi, with the profound humility that only a German movie director can summon, 'to sow in the Zone seeds of reality.'" Von Göll sees them simply as pieces in a chess game he controls. Each of these systems is futile; each lacks the control of reality it claims, and each deceives its creator.

Pynchon may believe, as several critics suggest, in an entropic vision of a world doomed to an eventual lack of order and energy. But he recognizes the presence of very important ordering systems at work in the world as we have it, systems which, even if ultimately doomed, pose a much more serious threat than those of individuals such as the Pointsman, von Göll, or even Weissmann. Unlike these systems, the "controlling" system rests not on individual delusion but on massive social forces which no single person directs. The system which Pynchon images as "They" involves a large number of individuals, most of whom do not consciously endorse the destruction they contribute to. Pirate Prentice, a well-meaning paratrooper capable of acting kindly, listens to Father Rapier's sermon on the nature of "They" and realizes that "with everything else, these are, after all, people who kill each other: and Pirate has always been one of them." The system, whether or not it reflects individual volition and/or an inherent order of reality, destroys human lives and reduces the survivors to unresisting accomplices.

Pynchon suggests one relatively simple technique for resisting Their pressure: reject Their categories, live on the interface between the terms of Their dichotomies. Roger Mexico, who contrasts directly with Pointsman, commits himself to life and love even when the commitment contradicts the statistical system with which he works: "If ever the Antipointsman existed, Roger Mexico is the man. Not so much, the doctor admits, for the psychical research. The young statistician is devoted to number and method, not table-rapping or wishful thinking. But in the domain of zero to one, not-something to something. Pointsman can only possess the zero and the one. He cannot, like Mexico, survive anyplace in between . . . to Mexico belongs the domain *between* zero and one — the middle Pointsman has excluded from his persuasion — the probabilities." The domain between one and zero, the interface between dream and reality, between self and society, the internal and the external, recurs frequently in *Gravity's Rainbow*. Denying the absolute validity of dichotomies — including that of realism and romance — results in a sense of common humanity as a weapon against the solipsism which insists on perceiving situations simply in either/or terms: "Kevin Spectro did not differentiate as much as he between Outside and Inside. He saw the cortex as an interface organ, meditating between the two, but *part of them both.* 'When you've looked at how it really is,' he asked once, 'how can any of us be separate?'"

Weakening the sense of separateness, existing on the interface, challenges our basic modes of perception. Pointsman observes that while we accept positions of certainty, yeses and nos, the process of transition frequently frightens us, as it does him, back into solipsistic isolation: "In each case, the change from point to no-point carries a luminosity and enigma at which something in us must leap and sing, or withdraw in fright." Nonetheless, as Mondaugen believes, the deepest life transpires precisely in that flow, that process of change:

> Think of the ego, the self that suffers a personal history bound to time, as the grid. The deeper and true Self is the flow between cathode and plate. The constant, pure flow. Signals—sense-data, feelings, memories relocating—are put onto the grid, and modulate the flow. We live lives that are waveforms constantly changing with time, now positive, now negative. Only at moments of great serenity is it possible to find the pure, the informationless state of signal zero.

To overcome our fear of the interface, we must break out of our solipsism. This struggle demands both Slothrop's recognition "that the Zone can sustain many other plots besides those polarized upon himself" and his later perception that the multiplicity of individual struggles is not taking place in a vacuum: "For the first time now it becomes apparent that the 4 and the Father-conspiracy do not entirely fill their world. Their struggle is not the only, or even the ultimate one. Indeed, not only are there many *other* struggles, but there are also *spectators,* watching, as spectators will do, hundreds of thousands of them." In essence, Slothrop learns to read the text of his *Gravity's Rainbow* in human rather than nihilistic terms. Most important, however, is the possibility of human contact which develops when two people find their way beyond the dichotomies and onto the interface at the same time and place: "Well. What happens when paranoid meets paranoid? A crossing of solipsisms. Clearly. The two patterns create a third: a moire, a new world of flowing shadows, interferences." Slothrop possesses something of this sense of possibility all along. Following his comic nightmare descent through the toilet, Slothrop finds himself on what he believes is the deepest level of his psyche. Expecting isolation, he discovers what appear to be archetypes: "only one fight, one victory, one loss. And only one president, and one assassin, and one election. True. One of each of everything. You had thought of solipsism, and imagined the structure to be populated—on your level—by only, terribly, one. No count on any other levels. But it proves to be not quite that lonely. Sparse, yes, but a good deal better than solitary. One of each of everything's not so bad." Soon Pynchon reveals even this degree of solipsistic isolation as an illusion:

> the plaza is seething with life, and Slothrop is puzzled. Isn't there
> supposed to be only one of each?
> A. Yes.
> Q. Then one Indian girl . . .
> A. One *pure* Indian. One *mestiza.* One *criolla.* Then: One Yaqui.
> One Navaho. One Apache—.

Obviously, if we pursue this path far enough, each of us is unique, each of us exists even on Slothrop's deepest solipsistic level of awareness. The secret lies in perceiving and accepting the similarity of our own isolation and that of others.

Gravity's Rainbow devotes a great deal of attention to those who fail to overcome their fear and perceive this bond, those who fall off the interface and commit themselves to solipsism. Such a commitment, Pynchon implies, inevitably contributes to Their system and results in physical and psychic death. While the end result may be the same, there are several different ways of retreating into solipsism. General Pudding, whose sexual life centers on eating and drinking Katje's excrement, provides the most striking example of the horrors of solipsism. His behavior, as Paul Fussell demonstrates, stems from his inability to confront the horror of World War I. He allows himself to degenerate into a perfect symbol of Their success in destroying human brotherhood in the twentieth century.

While Pudding provides the most extreme example, Major Duane Marvey, Franz Pökler, and Tchitcherine pursue lives leading to a similar dehumanization. Pökler believes he can remain personally removed from the immorality of the rocket-cartel system. However, "Pökler found that by refusing to take sides, he'd become Weissmann's best ally." Weissmann successfully manipulates Pökler, even while condemning Pökler's daughter to life in a concentration camp adjacent to the laboratory where her father works. Pökler's "neutrality," based on a naïve belief that integrity can survive without reference to external context, results in the very destruction he fears most.

Marvey and Tchitcherine share a fear of blackness which leads them to personal hells similar to Pökler's. The simpleminded Marvey sees blacks as bestial threats to American purity, while the more complex Tchitcherine reacts to his black half-brother Enzian as a threat to his personal sense of purity. Neither can accept any suggestion of a human bond with blackness, internal or external. Pynchon connects the inability of most whites in *Gravity's Rainbow,* and in Euro-American culture as a whole, to accept blackness with their (Their?) insistence on ignoring death:

> Shit, now, is the color white folks are afraid of. Shit is the presence of
> death, not some abstract-arty character with a scythe but the stiff and
> rotting corpse itself inside the whiteman's warm and private own

asshole, which is getting pretty intimate. That's what that white toilet's for. You see many brown toilets? Nope, toilet's the color of gravestones, classical columns of mausoleums, that white porcelain's the very emblem of Odorless and Official Death. Shinola shoeshine polish happens to be the color of Shit. Shoeshine boy Malcolm's in the toilet slappin' on the *Shinola,* working off whiteman's penance on his sin of being born the color of Shit 'n' Shinola.

Malcolm X's pursuit of Slothrop down the toilet, which ends with Slothrop in the solipsistic cesspool of his psychic sewer system, emphasizes the white tendency to dehumanize the self rather than accept the ambiguities of any relationship with blackness. While Slothrop recovers a sense of contact, at least in part, most whites in *Gravity's Rainbow* fail. Whether their solipsistic retreat stems from realistic social pressures (Marvey and Pudding) or individual symbolic reactions (Pökler and Tchitcherine), it aggravates both realistic and symbolic problems. By demonstrating the identical outcomes of apparently diverse situations, Pynchon effectively rejects the dichotomy between characters confronting experience on a realistic level and those confronting it on a symbolic level. The mode matters little. The human outcome demands attention.

In addition to the characters who surrender, Pynchon portrays several who struggle to escape their isolation and establish human contact. Significantly, the extent of their success has little to do with their theoretical beliefs. Roger Mexico, the statistician involved in a love affair with Jessica Swanlake, in unable to fit the experience into any of his "normal" categories of perception. "The time Roger and Jessica have spent together, totaled up, still only comes to hours. All their spoken words to less than one average SHAEF memorandum. And there is no way, first time in his career, that the statistician can make these figures mean anything. Together they are a long skin surface, flowing sweat, close as muscles and bones can press, hardly a word beyond her name or his. But he accepts the interface, the unquantifiable love he feels. Conversely, von Göll articulates the theory of human contact well: "Be compassionate. But don't make up fantasies about them. Despise me, exalt them, but remember, we define each other. Elite and preterite, we move through a cosmic design of darkness and light, and in all humility, I am one of the very few who can comprehend it *in toto.*" But his Daedalian arrogance leads him to force his aesthetic system onto life, leaving him with a perception of himself as one of the elite and negating any realistic application of his compassion.

Small acts of kindness glimmer through *Gravity's Rainbow.* In addition to Mexico's love for Jessica, Tantivy's loyalty to Slothrop, Bodine's gift of Dillinger's preterite blood and Katje's willingness to submit herself to the desperate needs of several lovers hint that some escape from solipsism into compassion is possible. The small gestures, however, dissolve frequently in frustration and at times generate new retreats into solipsism. Unable to separate herself from her fiance, Jeremy, Jessica abandons Roger after the immediate threat of the external war passes. Neither Tantivy nor Bodine saves Slothrop, Katje's shit kills Pudding.

The fate of the Hereros emphasizes the difficulties of realizing love and points out its tendency to collapse eventually into solipsism. The plot involving the Southwest African blacks who set up an independent rocket-oriented society within the Zone originates in the visit of Enzian's and Tchitcherine's Russian father to Africa in 1904. Old Tchitcherine, AWOL from a Russian ship, attains fleeting contact with a Herero girl: "It was nearly Christmas, and he gave her a medal he had won in some gunnery exercise long ago on the Baltic. By the time he left, they had learned each other's names and a few words in the respective languages—afraid, happy, sleep, love, . . . the beginnings of a new tongue, a pidgin which they were perhaps the only two speakers of in the world." Communication demands just this shared experience, a reaching beyond the self and a recognition that another shares both fears and joys. But their communication dissolves when Tchitcherine returns to Russia, leaving his lover and their child, Enzian, to the genocidal German policy. Enzian survives, eventually leading the *Schwarzkommando,* who seemingly promise a creative force counterbalancing the death-oriented Euro-American culture. But Enzian's vision of a redeemed rocket, a rocket of escape rather than of destruction, gradually generate a counterforce among the Hereros: the Empty Ones, devoted to tribal suicide. Preaching "a day when the last Zone-Herero will die, a final zero to a collective history fully lived," the Empty Ones are in fact defined by the very intensity of their opposition to European pressure. While symbolically their plan "has appeal," realistically it accomplishes exactly what Europeans from the Germans on most desire: the final repression of the black other. The original contact between old Tchitcherine and Enzian's mother simply extends the influence of the death-obsession to those blacks caught up in the political and psychological dichotomy of black and white.

Similarly, Slothrop's attempts to escape his solipsism ultimately fail. Despite his recognition of the bonds of humanity, despite his willingness to accept as full a range of reality as confronts him on whatever terms that confrontation generates, Slothrop simply dissolves. Neither his symbolic awareness nor acceptance of reality saves him. He falls victim to a sense of emptiness similar to that which affected Wyatt in *The Recognitions:* "If there is something comforting—religious, if you want—about paranoia, there is still also anti-paranoia, where nothing is connected to anything, a condition not many of us can bear for long. Well right now Slothrop feels himself sliding onto the anti-paranoid part of his cycle, feels the whole city around him going back roofless, vulnerable, uncentered as he is, and only pasteboard images now of the Listening Enemy left between him and the wet sky." Unlike Wyatt, however, Slothrop does not recover:

> Slothrop, as noted, at least as early as the *Anubis* era, has begun to thin, to scatter. "Personal density," Kurt Mondaugen in his Peene-münde office not too many steps away from here, enunciating the Law which will one day bear his name, "is directly proportional to temporal bandwidth." "Temporal bandwidth" is the width of your present, your *now*. It is the familiar "Δ t" considered as a dependent variable. The more you dwell in the past and in the future, the thicker your bandwidth, the more solid your persona. But the narrower your sense of Now, the more tenuous you are. It may get to where you're having trouble remembering what you were doing five minutes ago, or even — as Slothrop now — what you're doing *here*.

Soon he will be unnameable. Slothrop's disintegration reflects Pynchon's insistence that his characters cannot resolve the experiences of *Gravity's Rainbow*. Pynchon states the limitations of the characters directly:

> Who would have thought so many would be here? They keep appearing, all through this disquieting structure, gathered in groups, pacing alone in meditation, or studying the paintings, the books, the exhibits. It seems to be some very extensive museum, a place of many levels, and new wings that generate like living tissue — though if it all does grow toward some end shape, those who are here inside can't see it. Some of the halls are to be entered at one's peril, and monitors are standing at all the approaches to make this clear.

Rather than following the modernist approach by resolving *Gravity's Rainbow* through his own aesthetic structures (imposing his own perceptual system), Pynchon insists that, once we enter the halls, we find the exit for ourselves. He can offer us points of advice, guideposts, but they won't matter if we can't step outside our solipsism, first to confront the reality of *Gravity's Rainbow* and then to take it into our own lives.

When it matters most, Pynchon speaks to us directly. Using the second-person pronoun, Pynchon draws us into *Gravity's Rainbow;* our response depends on both our own experiences and our ability to empathize with others. Frequently, Pynchon attempts to make us participate in his vision through the use of traditional devices such as minutely detailed realistic settings or slapstick parody sequences written in third person. Having drawn us into his fictional world, Pynchon abruptly shifts to a direct form of address, reminding us that his world is also ours, demanding that we surrender our own solipsism and interact with the book. What Pynchon wants us to share, what he employs the second person to communicate, is his vision of a world of the preterite, a world in agony, a world in desperate need of love. The "you" passages occur throughout the book—there are some twenty in all—and when juxtaposed they challenge us to recognize the similarity of our own isolation and that of others, our share of responsibility for Their dominance, the serious consequences of giving in to isolation, and the necessity of extending ourselves to our brothers and sisters among the preterite in order to forge a new sense of moral community.

Slothrop's ancestor William wrote of the preterite as the source of moral value every bit as important as the elect: "'That's what Jesus meant,' whispers the ghost of Slothrop's first American ancestor William, 'venturing out of the Sea of Galilee. He saw it from the lemming point of view. Without the millions who had plunged and drowned, there could have been no miracle. The successful loner was only the other part of it: the last piece to the jigsaw puzzle, whose shape had already been created by the Preterite, like the last blank space on the table.'" Tyrone clings to the vision, extending it to our own world:

> Could he have been the fork in the road America never took, the singular point she jumped the wrong way from? Suppose the Sloth-ropite heresy had had the time to consolidate and prosper? Might there have been fewer crimes in the name of Jesus, and more mercy in the name of Judas Iscariot? It seems to Tyrone Slothrop that there might be a route back—maybe that anarchist he met in Zurich was right, maybe for a little while all the fences were down, one road as good as another, the whole space of the Zone cleared, depolarized, and somewhere inside the waste of it a single set of coordinates from which to proceed, without elect, without preterite, without even nationality to fuck it up.

Straining to break even the dichotomy of elect and preterite, Tyrone refuses simply to invert the terms and condemn the elect; preterition becomes a metaphor for the condition of all of us caught in systems based on arbitrary dichotomies.

Pynchon hymns of the preterite, reminding us of our own preterition, of

> men you have seen on foot and smileless in the cities but forget, men who don't remember you either, knowing they ought to be grabbing a little sleep, not out here performing for strangers, give you this evensong, climaxing now with its rising fragment of some ancient scale, voices overlapping three—and fourfold, up, echoing, filling the entire hollow of the church—no counterfeit baby, no announcement of the Kingdom, not even a try at warming or lighting this

terrible night, only, damn us, our scruffy obligatory little cry, our maximum reach outward—*praise be to God!*—for you to take back to your war-address, your war-identity, across the snow's footprints and tire tracks finally to the path you must create by yourself, alone in the dark. Whether you want it or not, whatever seas you have crossed, the way home.

He writes of "Your own form immobile, mouth-breaking, alone face-up on the narrow cot next to the wall so pictureless, chartless, mapless: so *habitually blank*." He places us on the target as the rocket descends, staring up with Pökler to confront the physical symbol of the destructive effect of our own attempts to remain uninvolved:

> Now what sea is this you have crossed, exactly, and what sea is it you have plunged more than once to the bottom of, alerted, full of adrenalin, but caught really, buffaloed under the epistemologies of these threats that paranoid you so down and out, caught in this steel pot, softening to devitaminized mush inside the soup-stock of your own words, your waste submarine breath? It took the Dreyfus Affair to get the Zionists out and doing, finally: what will drive you out of your soup-kettle? Has it already happened? Was it tonight's attack and deliverance? Will you go to the Heath, and begin your settlement, and wait there for your Director to come?

He forces us either to retreat to solipsism or to share the agony, and the responsibility for the agony. If we refuse to see ourselves in the "you" Pynchon addresses, we aren't going to get much out of *Gravity's Rainbow*.

All we have, finally, is love. It may be too much to expect, but nothing's more important than trying to find, to love:

> You have waited in these places into the early mornings, synced in to the on-whitening of the interior, you know the Arrivals schedule by heart, by hollow heart. And where these children have run away from, and that, in this city, there is no one to meet them. You impress them with your gentleness. You've never quite decided if they can see through to your vacuum. They won't yet look in your eyes.
> . . . Tonight's child has had a long trip here, hasn't slept. Her eyes are red, her frock wrinkled. Her coat has been a pillow. You feel her exhaustion, feel the impossible vastness of all the sleeping countryside at her back, and for the moment you really are selfless, sexless . . . considering only how to shelter her, you are the Traveler's Aid.

If nothing else, we can shelter strangers. Occasionally we can love like Mexico loves Jessica. Pynchon pulls us deeper than direct address at the end of section one of *Gravity's Rainbow*. He has spoken to us. Here we speak to Jessica. There are no quotation marks, no Joycean distancing techniques. Living under attack, we merge with Mexico: "You go from dream to dream inside me. You have passage to my last shabby corner, and there, among the debris, you've found life. I'm no longer sure which of all the words, images, dreams or ghosts are 'yours' and which are 'mine.' It's past sorting out. We're both being someone new now, someone incredible." Pynchon offers us a "we" which can include Roger, Jessica, Pynchon, you and me. Recognizing the fragility, we share our cry with Mexico: "You're catching the War. It's infecting you and I don't know how to keep it away. Oh, Jess. Jessica. Don't leave me . . ."

She leaves.

Just as Pynchon refuses to offer us a traditional resolution through Slothrop, he refuses to offer us a vicarious resolution through Mexico. If we love, we love in reality, not on a printed page. We love with our dreams and our bodies, but we love together, not alone with our books. The last words are Pynchon's: "All together now, all you masochists out there, specially those of you don't have a partner tonight, alone with those fantasies that don't look like they'll ever come true—want you just to join in here with your brothers and sisters, let each other know you're alive and sincere, try to break through the silences, try to reach through and connect."

Now Everybody.

Creative Paranoia and Frost Patterns of White Words

Gabriele Schwab

> *It is not expected of critics as it is of poets that they should help us to make sense of our lives; they are bound only to attempt the lesser feat of making sense of the ways we try to make sense of our lives.*
>
> —FRANK KERMODE

On April 24, 1985, the *New York Times* published an article by James Markham under the headline "West German TV Specials Spark Debate Over the Nazi Era," which contained the following passage: "Directors and scriptwriters deny suggestions of revisionism and say, rather, that they want to explore the subtle appeals of Nazism, the way it looked in microcosm and how the machinery of war functioned on both sides. They say they represent the members of a postwar generation trying to make sense of their parents' war."

The very idea of trying to make sense of this war all of a sudden struck me as having something utterly inappropriate and uncanny about it. Yet, at the same time, it also seemed to lie at the core of the speeches given in the course of the then ongoing debates over President Reagan's visit to the German cemetery at Bitburg in West Germany. The rhetoric used to defend his visit to a place where more than forty SS soldiers are buried, made one wonder if the project of making sense of World War II and its war crimes is not to some extent inevitably condemned to a kind of involuntary complicity, to defensiveness and rationalization. The language used in what the *New York Times* quite appropriately called "Search

---

From *Making Sense.* © 1986 by Fink Verlag, Munich. Originally entitled "Creative Paranoia and Frost Patterns of White Words: Making Sense in and of *Gravity's Rainbow.*"

for Meaning at Bitburg" (headline on May 6, 1985) became extremely vulnerable to unwanted overtones which spoke, in a displacement of meaning, literally but unknowingly of the unspeakable. "Out of the ashes—hope" was the uncanny cover banner of *Time Magazine,* quoting the message delivered by the President during his performances at Bergen-Belsen and Bitburg. This message, spread by the media all over the world, evokes the archetype of a rebirth out of destruction and death. But how comfortable can we feel with this archetype in the face of the concrete extinction and the ashes of millions of Jews, and also of communists, gypsies and mentally ill people, on which this hope is built? There is no room left for "innocent" metaphors after these artrocities—even if one does not go as far as Adorno who asserts that Auschwitz affects the very status of any poetry that comes after it.

What then is the status of a historical fiction like *Gravity's Rainbow* which deals with World War II? How does it confront the problem of making sense? Amazingly enough, the epigraph to *Gravity's Rainbow* also evokes the archetype of a rebirth out of destruction. "Nature does not know extinction; all it knows is transformation," quotes a message of hope, too, a prophecy of transcendence, added by Wernher von Braun to his legacy of "the bomb." This very archetype of destruction and renewal forms the basis for the most pertinent, and often perverse collective phantasies shared by numerous characters in *Gravity's Rainbow.* But instead of delivering a message of hope, the novel itself builds up a dramatic tension with respect to its characters' phantasies, leaving it up to the reader to make sense of the apocalyptic frame. One of the reasons I was captured by Pynchon's novel was precisely that it seemed to refuse to make sense, or that at least it made sense otherwise, that it was so unlike any other historical fiction I had read about World War II. Being born "after the war" in Germany, I approached *Gravity's Rainbow* as the fiction of a past which my generation, facing the deadly silence of its participants, has tried to approach, if not to exorcise, through documents—history books, novels, films, letters.

When this postwar generation entered the university in the Sixties, the Vietnam war became the displaced scene from which to confront both its own history and war in general. The author of *Gravity's Rainbow,* published in 1973 when the Vietnam war and the radical movements of the Sixties were coming to an end, had himself gathered his knowledge about World War II mainly from periodical source-texts such as *The London Times* of 1944–45, as well as from films, history books, and literary and theoretical texts. In a way, then, this novel is "about" both wars, though its fictional time focuses primarily on the years 1944 and 1945. In another way, it does not seem to be a historical novel about World War II at all, nor really satire on the Sixties in America. It seems rather a fiction reflecting theories and concepts that emerged in the forties but shape our minds today, a historical gaze upon the present that blends different historical epochs and literary language games together. Poems of Rainer Maria Rilke, films by Fritz Lang, and operas by Wagner, styles and scenes from historical novels, science fiction, spy novels, comics, and musicals — all inform the novel's notion of history as well as its ever-changing modulations of language. Moreover, theoretical intertexts derived from cybernetics, physics, and communication theory amalgamate historical events with their respective systems of knowledge and their widespread influence.

No wonder, then, that instead of recognizing a World War II scenario familiar from other sources, one might rather feel catapulted into a science fiction space. There is, of course, London in the mid-forties, a precise historical location, and there are other scattered elements that might be traced back to historical facts, but in the reading process, these elements of a conventional historical novel are easily absorbed by the exoticism and superabundance of grotesque and surreal scenes. One loses track of history in meeting with such characters as psychic Captain Prentice who has other people's dreams, Tyrone Slothrop who responds sexually to Hitler's V-2, the Adenoid, a lymphatic monster "as big as St. Paul's," or the giant octopus Grigori, trained in the Secret Service. History seems to have been made or mystified by new gnostics, electromysticists, Zone Hereros, or even by a Walt Disney-inspired immortal light bulb called Byron, who inhabits a "purified Electroworld."

With his unbelievably fantastic stories and eccentric characters, Pynchon seems to have moved away from historiography to archeology, unearthing madness, perversity, and monstrosity at the margins and beneath the surface of history. He blurs familiar boundaries between segmented histories — politics, economics, technology, science, religion, art, popular culture, or individual lives. Scientific or political information, historical "facts" in fictional guise, philosophies and archaic mythologies are fused. Theories such as Norbert Wiener's cybernetics, Werner Heisenberg's uncertainty principle, or Henry Adams' social entropy are combined with an abundant range of art works from poetry, comics, films, operas, and musicals. Different epochs, cultures and styles are presented through a mixing of codes, while the narrator often disperses into an echo of "alien voices" borrowed from these codes.

Foucault, Bakhtin, and the early Barthes could have inspired this archeological and carnivalistic approach to history in *Gravity's Rainbow,* which has been called an "encyclopedic novel." I would prefer to call it an "ecological fiction" for it is precisely *not* an accumulation of knowledge but rather the unification and interrelation of commonly isolated areas of experience that convey the notion of history. This recalls, in fact, Gregory Bateson's *Steps to an Ecology of Mind* which deals with the negative effects of subdividing a culture by isolating areas of experience or research. Processes of isolating certain areas of experience such as history, or literature, are of course necessary for any attempt at comprehension. They are basic operations of the mind to reduce the complexity of an environment by ordering it. Order itself is a result of segmentation which imprints itself into our very modes of perception. According to Bateson, the problem is that we tend to perceive our categories of order as real subdivisions of our world instead of understanding them as mere "*abstractions* which we make for our own convenience when we set out to describe cultures in words"; "we must expect that any single trait of a culture will prove on examination to be not simply economic or religious or structural but to partake of all these qualities according to the point of view from which we look at it. If this be true of a culture seen in synchronic section, then it must also apply to the diachronic processes of culture contact and change."

Bateson's ecological notion of history and culture helps us to understand the organization of the fictional world in *Gravity's Rainbow* as well as its notion of history and its aesthetic devices. Any historical novel has to make choices as to what it presents as central to the epoch or the culture it reconstructs as a fictional world. Conventionally, historical novels convey their notion of history through the lives of heroic characters whose experiences were told in allegorical, or—as we would prefer to say today—paradigmatic narratives. But with the growing epistemological suspicion against this kind of narrative, a suspicion that has affected the writing of history and literature alike, the historical novel faces a challenge affecting its very modes of representation.

Gravity's Rainbow meets this challenge with various aesthetic devices:

1. The text refuses to center on a few hypostatized characters, or even a few exemplary plots. By ironically labeling the level of plot and character "secular history," the novel suggests that the main plots of history are staged by transpersonal agencies of power, whereas the characters perform subplots that serve these agencies in various ways. This polarizing of different levels of history is mediated by a narrator who is able to shift between the two, and who can therefore function as a guiding figure for the reader.

2. The novel undermines a purely chronological, linear view of history by inserting fragments of past and future into the more narrowly defined historical frame. This culminates in the projection of history as a simultaneous time-scenario.

3. The text avoids the segmentation of domains by incorporating the history of science, technology, literature, religion, and popular culture into the body of political history and personal stories. It displays its intertextuality as a historical device, aimed at a reconstruction of historical knowledge that recognizes

the profound influence of the media on the making of history and subjectivity, as well as the influence of other texts on the making of *Gravity's Rainbow*.

4. The novel generates a new type of reading by training the ability to shift more flexibly between different levels of perception and abstraction, and by reactivating multidimensional levels of thought.

5. The text contains an implicit utopia of an accumulated historical memory that is itself multidimensional and that would undermine any attempt at making sense of history by closing off certain areas of experience from their environmental influences. As a consequence, the reader will not find a meaning in *Gravity's Rainbow*. Making sense of the text will instead require and train faculties that resist prefabricated messages and favor readings against the grain.

In the following pages, I want to pursue these assumptions in more detail. One of the distinctive features of the ecological notion of history in *Gravity's Rainbow* is a blurring of boundaries between domains which we have become accustomed to perceive as separate. Such transgressions of conventional boundaries are, of course, not specific to *Gravity's Rainbow*, but characteristic of postmodern literature in general. And there are also theories of history which favor such transgressions on an epistemological basis. But in *Gravity's Rainbow* these new modes of presenting history assume a specific importance because it is a historical novel about World War II. This very subject matter becomes a touchstone for some of our most cherished contemporary epistemological assumptions.

We have, for example, become used to accepting greater and greater blurrings of the boundaries between reality and fiction. But in the context of a historical novel about World War II such blurrings appear in a different light. The way in which *Gravity's Rainbow* links history to performance or reality to fiction is utterly provocative because of its ambiguities. "It's all theatre," according to Pirate Prentice's vision at the beginning of the novel, the invisible crashing of the V-2, the Evacuation, the everyday horrors of the war. Spy dramas on the political stage control the melodramas of interpersonal relationships. Does Pynchon, then, free us from the "gravity" of reality by dispersing it into the free play of the "simulacrum"?

This can hardly be the case, because there is, for example, a decisive political criticism of van Goell's *Alpdruecken,* a film which creates a collective dream used by characters such as Franz Poekler to derealize reality or to aestheticize politics. Walter Benjamin has shown how the creation of film stars as symbols of a collective dream *(Kollektivtraum)* can be used as a kind of vaccination that induces a therapeutic explosion of the unconscious. Greta Erdmann is such a film star on whom numerous men are said to have fathered their imaginary children, but the very title of the film in which she stars, *Alpdruecken,* meaning nightmare, is a hint of the dark side of those collective dreams, which is, moreover, reinforced by the portrayal of a Greta Erdmann who, in her real life, mutilates Jewish boys. The portrayal of characters in *Gravity's Rainbow* demonstrates that the production of collective dreams by films does not necessarily induce the cathartic reaction which Walter Benjamin foregrounds in his analysis. Just as often it provides a frame of meaning that allows the characters to indulge in a pornography of violence. Interpersonal violence, sadomasochism, and sexual degradation seem to transfer some of the destructive energies of the war into the private sphere. But this results in a dangerous analogy of the private and the public, the handling of which requires a delicate act of aesthetic balance. In this respect, there is a certain ambiguity in Pynchon's novel, and I am not sure if his portrayal of characters always manages to avoid the trap of trivializing politics and history by taking the microcosmic perspective of those involved in them. My reading is an effort at making the text as strong as possible. But I retain a certain uneasiness as to its implicit analysis of fascism. There has been, after all, a dubious and frightfully successful marketing of fascism—especially of Hitler himself—that has often been based on deadly facile analogies, ranging from fantasies of erotic encounters between the male Nazi brute and the beautiful Jewish victim to numerous attempts at reducing the threatening complexities of fascism through an analysis of Hitler's relationship with his mother.

The characters in *Gravity's Rainbow* themselves have recourse to a whole range of possible systems which might provide them with a meaning for their shattering experiences. Most of them verge on mysticism, nurturing hopes of transcendence. The Tarot, ESP, mystical death cults, Spiritism, and Zen Buddhism are not antagonistic counterparts to the dominating technology of war, but on the contrary, means to anthropomorphize it by infusions of mystical meaning. One aspect of this coupling of technology and mysticism in *Gravity's Rainbow* can also be understood in ecological terms. The fictional reconstruction of history shows how the one could not function without the other. Male technology, pertaining, in the characters' own words, to a system of death and control, needs the anima of mysticism quite literally as an animating force. Otherwise it could not invade human subjectivity, which it needs to ground and exert its historical power.

Linguistically, this process is enhanced by Pynchon's use of strong root metaphors that bring the commonly different systems of reference—technology and mysticism—into contiguity or proximity. The latter might be experienced as a collision or as a *unio mystica*. In both cases the metaphors are generative by conveying or supporting a notion of subjectivity that could not be gained with reference to either of the systems alone.

On the other hand, this very coupling of technology and mysticism is shown to be one of the forces that keeps the war machinery going. It allows the characters to mystify politics and history—a mystification they eagerly embrace as a defense mechanism, a denial of reality. Making sense of a technology of destruction by implanting hopes of mystical transcendence in it is revealed as a self-destructive cathexis.

One could see this as a form of "aestheticizing politics." Benjamin, who introduced this term in order to describe the effects of fascist propaganda, stressed the tremendous impact of the media in the fulfillment of the political aims of fascism. In the media the masses could, for the first time, find an expression of themselves as part of a grandiose spectacle of the performative aspects of the war that contributed to the formation of a collective subjectivity. Pynchon, however, focuses on still another form of aestheticizing politics: the production of collective dreams and rationalizing mythologies. "All efforts to render politics aesthetic culminate in one thing: war" (Benjamin). This holds true for the propagandistic representation of the masses in the media as well as for the rationalization of violence in collective dreams. From this perspective, it becomes clear that if there is a postmodern text which makes it totally obsolete to blur the distinction between reality and representation, this text is *Gravity's Rainbow*. It reestablishes the difference between the two on a macrolevel precisely because its characters blur it on a microlevel in a tacit complicity with fascist mystifications. Thus, Pynchon introduces a new level of differentiation. It is true that each representation of reality produces reality and can therefore no longer be perceived as separate from it. But it is also true that one has to reintroduce a difference between the two on a higher level of abstraction if one wants to escape from mystifying representations.

Such representations are to be found on every level of experience. In *Gravity's Rainbow* the fictionalization of fact is shown to be as much a reality as is the factualization of fictions. The fusion of the real and the imaginary is a strategy used on both personal and transpersonal levels. This is why the novel no longer focuses on historical facts. Whether in the paranoid melodramas of the characters' lives, in the cybernetic formation of their imaginary personalities, in the coupling of technology with mythology, in the accumulated memories of protagonists whose mediated vision of the war was already conditioned by literature and film, or in the accumulated memory of the novel itself whose author, eight years old in 1945, has taken his historical material from films and letters— in all these phenomena we face the imagery and theatrical elements of the war. It is therefore impossible to continue to see myth or fiction and their relation to reality in terms of part and whole. Fictions and myths, theatre and performance are so basic to the psychopolitics of war that they can no longer be relegated to the margin of historiography, and Pynchon has, in fact, placed them in the center as elements of "the very machinery that made the war operate."

But at the same time, the novel makes it clear that in order to understand this very historical condition we have to retain the means and train the capacity to differentiate between qualitatively different representations of reality on a higher level of abstraction. By inviting us to follow the narrator in shifting between a microlevel of plots and individual stories, and a macrolevel with a different organization of history, Pynchon lures us to step out of habitualized ways of perceiving history. The reading process would thus ideally resemble processes of reframing as described by Erving Goffman or therapeutic escapes from reality constraints by shifts to a metalevel as described by Gregory Bateson. Both Goffman and Bateson stress the fact that we have to be trained to perceive the abstractions of reality as abstractions (instead of mistaking them for reality as such) in order to change them.

At the same time, Pynchon shows the entanglement in self-fabricated or collectively produced abstractions of reality as formative for the subjectivity of historical subjects. The reframing of subjectivity, then, becomes a project of resistance against petrification. On the other hand, the experience of war is shown to favor such petrifications. The daily exposure to destruction, death, war crimes, or sexual perversities seems to engender both derealizing and simplifying strategies of making sense and of making selves. Defensively, the characters turn Rilke into the guru of a mystifying death-drive, Wagner and Humperdinck into soap operas of apocalypse and transcendence. Every mythology is robbed of its internal differentiation, reduced to psychological clichés, cultural waste, or raw formulas of vulgar philosophies of life. The anthropomorphization of technology symbolized by the mystified "Rocket" allows the characters to veil the petrification of automatized humans and their collective, lemming-like "war-drive."

From this perspective "it's all theatre," indeed, the theatre of "imaginary personalities" who choose to live out their illusions of reality. Blindfolded characters take refuge in mythologies, starring in them as active performers on a historical stage which is, in fact, just as much directed by "alien forces," by transpersonal systems of control. These are shown to be the real agents of history that control and exploit even collective dreams and mythologies: the "White Visitation," a biomedical research center that experiments with "human material," "IG Farben," the firm that produces "Kryptosam" administered to Slothrop, "ACHTUNG," the "Allied Clearing House, Technical Units, Northern Germany," and many more.

These transpersonal agencies are too complex to become transparent for the characters, but from a macroperspective one sees the two as constantly interacting. The characters have a sense of the power of transpersonal systems, and they even participate in it, sometimes unwillingly, sometimes unknowingly. But in order to incorporate their effects into systems of belief, the characters tend to anthropomorphize them through myths of extinction and transcendence. They even reveal a will to remain oblivious of the degree to which they themselves act out "historical happenings" on a stage, where the boundaries between the real and the imaginary are blurred in a deceitful self-protection against death, chaos, and extinction. The transpersonal systems are perceived as a new kind of Leviathan which depends on human subjects to play his game, but which, at the same time, shapes the very fabric of their subjectivity, impregnating them with more and more of his alien substance. Warfare as such becomes an abstraction experienced on the same level as other transpersonal systems. It reactivates the metaphor of the human automaton. The individual is consumed as part and material of the war machinery, and this machinery even expands its boundaries by means of chemical, biological, or genetic manipulations. At the same time, the mutilated remains of individuality sound the retreat into perverted shapes of ancient archetypal mythologies, humanistic nostalgia, or the metaphysics of individuality. But even those mythologies are generated as much by modern technologies and their modes of information as by disowned or violated individual histories. The two are always already intertwined. Subjectivity has become that of human "cyborgs," cybernetic organisms, of whom Tyrone Slothrop, having undergone a literal cybernetification of the human body, is the uncanny prototype.

Even the nostalgic revival of ancient myths of transcendence is subjugated to the technological imagination, thus enforcing rather than opposing the fabrication of cyborg subjectivities. The cyborg seems, in fact, to be the true child of the coupling of technology and mysticism, and the new wave of bringing the two together in the Sixties reveals the actuality of a cybernetic notion of subjectivity not only for the historical but also for the actual context of Pynchon's novel. Kurt Mondaugen's new wave electromysticism, for example, accommodates familiar notions of the self to the dynamic of technology, and I see this as an attempt to understand the self according to the new electronic age:

> Think of the ego, the self that suffers a personal history bound to time, as the grid. The deeper and true Self is the flow between cathode and plate . . . We live lives that are waves—forms constantly changing in time, now positive, now negative. Only at moments of great serenity is it possible to find the pure, the informationless state of signal zero.
>
> [Gravity's Rainbow]

The mechanization and cybernetification of the human body and mind are informed by a technological eros. Historically, this is of course related to the eroticized cathexis of technology by the Futurists. "War is beautiful because it initiates the dreamt-of metalization of the human body," wrote Marinetti in his manifesto on the Ethiopian colonial war. Here, the aesthetization of politics extends its effects to the production of subjectivity. The specific metaphors Pynchon uses to grasp these effects reveal a transition from the human automaton, which was a product of the mechanical age, to the cyborg as a product of the new age of electrical-electronic technologies. The human automaton and the cyborg seem to be collective phantasies which are used like transitional objects or phenomena to symbolize a transition in the historical formation of subjectivity. The human automaton, which symbolized the transition between romantic and modern subjectivity, is replaced by the cyborg which symbolizes the transition to postmodern forms of subjectivity. The human automaton was created as a centered organism and as such served to compensate for the uncontrollable forces of the unconscious at the price of a shift to the inanimate. Pynchon's cyborgs, on the other hand, are decentered in a new way. Cybernetic organisms are manipulated as much by transindividual semiotic systems as they are driven by individual desires, and the interplay between the two produces an implosion of complexity that reaches beyond individual consciousness. The traditional "know thyself" can therefore no longer be restricted to individual consciousness. Pynchon seems to suggest that it will have to be revealed in the analysis of cyborg subjectivities.

This aesthetic presentation of cyborgs, based on a new concept of subjectivity, is of course crucial for the status of all processes of making sense both in and of *Gravity's Rainbow*. The invasion of mechanical, electronic, mathematical, or chemical metaphors into self- and world-imageries, far from being fancy rhetoric, indicates that not only the "social body" *(corps social)* but "mindbodies" themselves are infiltrated by the alien bodies of technology. Even warlike human automatons reemerge as archaic regressions among the cyborgs. Characters like Blicero, Gottfried, Enzian, Tchitcherine, or Pointsman have acquired an eroticized metal ego. Fusing symbolically with their weapons or even with their function in the war machine, they become "transformer-selves," very much like the "transformers" you could buy as the favored toys for American boys in 1984 — soldiers metamorphosing into guns, robots into tanks, and the American Adam into He-Man, the master of the universe. Here the equation turns uncanny. Pynchon screens the American dream as an extension of what resulted in the nightmare of World War II, or, as Paul Fussell has formulated it: "Memory haunts Pynchon's novel. Its shape is determined by a 'memory' of the Second War, specifically the end of it and its immediate aftermath, when it is beginning to modulate into the Third."

Gottfried, whose naked body is tied to the womb of the V-2, allegorizes a collective masculine death-drive with all its misogynist implications. Blicero's ritualistic firing of the Rocket with its sacrificial victim is a technologically inspired reenactment of the mythological "Great Mother." The latter is, in fact a crucial stereotype in the psychohistory of male technological fantasies. As "Hi-Tech-Supermom," she has been resurrected in various American space rockets, engendering the collective dream of "Star Wars" as a military technological program, a displaced battlefield for acting out anxieties that revolve around the cruise missiles of menacing World War III as much as those of Pynchon's characters revolve around the V-2.

By superimposing contemporary American visions and scenes onto a World War II scenario, Pynchon has created a "simultaneous fiction." Apart from suggesting that the Second World War is, as Paul Fussell has pointed out, already beginning to modulate into the Third, this fiction inserts the present into the past. Malcolm X, John F. Kennedy, Richard Nixon, or even Plasticman are "foreign bodies" smuggled into an alien historical frame. But the simultaneity of the fiction is much more radical than a mere intertextual play. It feigns a conceivable unity of one historical picture that would encompass past, present, and future in an order that is neither chronological nor hierarchical. In this respect it resembles the timelessness of dream images. In other respects, however, it is unlike the dream image because its order does not derive from primary processes but from secondary processes. The production of such a picture is possible because the use of high-tech media allows the projection of time-scenarios which might well take the place of history, for they create a kind of transhistorical storage of history. Thus the totality of historical time could be produced at any moment, and this reconstruction of history would blur the distinction between diachronic and synchronic orders of time. The time structure of *Gravity's Rainbow* — its simultaneity — and the perspective of the narrator both anticipate the possibility of reconstructions of history that would select their material out of such time-scenarios instead of following more conventional notions of chronology.

This utopian dimension in *Gravity's Rainbow,* implicit in both the hypostasis of cyborglike subjectivities and the projection of a simultaneous time-scenario, is perhaps the most radical, but not the dominant feature in Pynchon's historical fiction. It is used as a demystifying device on the macrolevel to counterbalance the mystifying representations of history in which the characters are entangled. But there is another demystifying device, on the microlevel, which is likely to be even more effective during the reading process itself. It is a specific kind of carnivalization of history, effective not only on the level of the novel's intertextuality with popular culture but also practiced by those characters who, towards the end of the novel, founded the "Counterforce," an exotic bunch of former double agents, members of the "Schwarzkommando" and other "preterites." Historically, they are inspired by the vanguard movement of the Weimar Republic, by Dadaism and Surrealism which are, simultaneously, telescoped into Pop Art and the Dada of the Sixties.

Dada was directed against the spirit of gravity, "gravitas," practicing, like the Counterforce, an "art of militant irony." Highly ambivalent towards its own era and towards fascism, Dadaism was a movement that oscillated between aestheticizing affirmation and unconditional opposition. Polemically directed against Expressionism, and especially against Rilke—who, in *Gravity's Rainbow*, inspires Blicero's mystification of the Rocket—Dada also cherished the principle of historical simultaneity. But instead of creating a utopian time-scenario, Dada rejected the very idea of order and teleology, and explored the designifying potential of meaningless contingencies. But, like the Counterforce and the Dada of the Sixties, Dada also indulged in ecstasies of destruction, which was enhanced by a desperate anticipation of its unavoidable failure.

The resistance of the Counterforce, to which Pynchon dedicated the last book of the novel, shows the pleasures of an ostentatiously staged and unbounded infantile regression mobilized against the fear of inevitable extermination. Rejecting both a fatal reality principle and compensatory mythologies, the Counterforce does not aim at a transcendence to pure being but at a "transcendence downward" into a world of farcical insignificance. Refusing to make sense of what should and cannot make sense, it hurls its sense-contaminations, its "non-sense" against a mythologizing semiotization of the war. At a "Gross Suckling Conference" the members of the Counterforce exhibit themselves as victimized children of a society that acts like a "great mother" who feeds, clothes, and finally devours them because what some still perceive as "systemic rationality" has gone mad and destructive.

The members of the Counterforce are the only characters in the novel who initiate a movement against annihilation. Significantly, it is itself ambivalent, limited in scope and unable to avoid the disasters of war. But just as significantly, it uses designifying strategies—that old weapon of the hopelessly inferior resistance—against an overwhelming mystified and horrifying reality.

One could venture to see *Gravity's Rainbow* itself as an "aesthetic counterforce," but the facile analogy grasps only some of the novel's aspects. The amalgamation of the most sophisticated art forms with the crudest ingredients of mass-cultural waste is certainly a post modern form of carnivalization that creates an aesthetic counterforce. And the infiltration of World War II scenarios with both archaic as well as contemporary mythologies functions like Bakhtin's reconstruction of an acting, accumulated memory. Inaccessible to a linear or chronological historical narrative, this memory needs to be expressed by a simultaneous fiction that functions just as do those numerous Pynchonesque "interfaces," like a "zone of contact" (Bakhtin) between times and spaces.

The concept of history as simultaneous fiction is further supported by the skillfully interwoven theoretical intertexts. Heisenberg's quantum theory, and Derrida's critique of Western metaphysics are invoked to introduce Pynchon's hobbyhorse — entropy — the key concept that informs the narrative, structure, style, and implicit philosophy of *Gravity's Rainbow*. Pynchon suggests entropic processes may exist on every level of human experience, but he introduces a narrator who — not without self-irony — views and orders the entropic dissolutions from outside. He does so by simulating a four-dimensional perspective which includes past, present, and future and which can clearly be seen as a negentropic force because it opens an otherwise closed system. Ironically however, this very perspective enforces the impression of entropy on the level of the experience of reading. For the reader will not spontaneously shift to a four-dimensional perspective but tends instead to remain, like the characters themselves, entangled in the linear development of plots. The strategy of multiple perspectives thus adds to the overwhelming complexity which is not easily reduced to an order. But the narrator repeatedly invites and enables a shift to a four-dimensional perspective which requires an effort to go beyond internalized habits of perception. Thus Pynchon's aesthetic devices generate, in fact, a new type of reading. Seen from a four-dimensional perspective, the playful simulation of entropy challenges the reader's three-dimensional frame of mind. The internalized pattern of space, time, and causality that underlie our notions of history seem to dissolve into the contingencies of exuberantly growing stories. The experience of contingency, or entropy, can only be compensated for by a shift to a higher level of order.

The deliberately induced loss of orientation, and the strategies that help the reader to overcome it constructively, have a utopian dimension insofar as they anticipate aesthetically future developments in writing and thought that have also surfaced in theoretical speculations. The French archeologist André Leroi-Gourhan has advanced the idea of a transition to four-dimensional thinking, later taken up in Derrida's *Grammatology*. According to Leroi-Gourhan, the technological developments in our so-called computer age will replace our linear, writing-centered thinking by multidimensional thought processes and practices that require a reactivation of preverbal, simultaneous, and associative modes of perception.

Thomas Pynchon was among the first to face this challenge in a novel which is nevertheless bound to writing and was written for "three-dimensional readers." Thus he contributes, in his own playful way, to leading us a step further into the differentiation of our own cyborglike subjectivity. Intertextual and intertemporal devices provide Pynchon with a literary form for a multidimensional concept of history and the self. These devices allow the reader to experience a different time-order and an ecological interdependency of historical phenomena *within* the two-dimensional framework of writing *(écriture)* and the linear order of print. If we want to make sense of *Gravity's Rainbow,* we have to learn to shift between these different orders.

The most radical implication of this new historical vision is perhaps the idea that the old "secular history" is a "diversionary tactic" *(GR)* which blinds us to the economics and technology of war. Pynchon seems to suggest that the transpersonal agencies assert their power through the channels of a traditional notion of history, and that we have to see beyond if we want to perceive and perhaps change "the persistence of structures favoring death" *(GR).*

This is where the new historical novel unfolds both an apocalyptic and an implicit utopian dimension. It suggests that apocalyptic myths of the Rocket or the cosmic bomb, as much as the actual occurrence of megadeath, pertain to a secular history staged by transpersonal agents as an "other scene" (I see an affinity here, on the level of a "political unconscious," to Freud's "other scene" of the dream). The dangerous ambiguity is that even this notion can be appropriated by strategies of denial that allow those involved in the war to reject their own responsibility. This is how one of the fascists tries to place himself beyond "History": "The mass nature of wartime death is useful in many ways. It serves as spectacle, as diversion from the real movements of the war. It provides raw material to be recorded into History as sequences of violence, battle after battle" *(GR).*

Gravity's Rainbow makes our dwelling in mystified "secular histories" as obsolete as the facile counterreaction implied in the notion that we are "beyond history." The text reveals that the "other scene" of history can also be that of the "political unconscious," hidden from secular history, which one can only reveal if history is read against the grain. One project of *Gravity's Rainbow* is to invite such a reading, and in this respect, too, it is an archeology more than a historiography. In the context of the two juxtaposed historical stages, the novel about the apocalyptic Rocket turns into an "experimental" or a "second degree mythology" as defined by Roland Barthes, a mythology that demystifies because it is transplanted into a self-reflexive context. That is why *Gravity's Rainbow* is not an apocalyptic fiction, but an apocalyptic metafiction. And, as we are never to forget, it is a carnivalistic show subversive of its own totalizing tendencies. Its end is a "descent," a "final countdown" in San Francisco's Orpheus Theater, initiated by the audience's rhythmical chant "Come on! Start-the-show!" *(GR).* But the show is the silent fall of the apocalyptic Rocket on the imaginary world as stage whose end is to be invented by the reader. And yet: the end of *history* is beyond the end of *Gravity's Rainbow.*

How, then, does *Gravity's Rainbow* make sense? Precisely by refusing to make sense in the way conventional historical novels do. On the one hand, the text focuses on processes of making sense that were effective for (or made effective by) those involved in its fictional presentation of war—the paranoid melodramas or theatrical performances of the literary characters. As Paul Fussell has argued, the theatrical element was actually an indispensible means of inducing men to perform in the war. By foregrounding war mythologies as raw facts of the war, Pynchon reveals the full obscenity of making sense of war in a totalizing way. By subverting these mythologies through numerous intertextual and carnivalistic devices, he leaves the text open, refusing to make sense of World War II, refusing to even allow it to be primarily *about* World War II. The novel deliberately ends with unresolved ambiguities.

Thus it is up to the reader to make sense of the novel. In a first reading it is most likely that one will be lost in the complexities, intransparencies, and contingencies of this text, which approaches us subliminally. In order to transform this reading into an experience that makes sense we might—like some of the characters—take refuge in the protecting shapes of mythologies, be they derived from archaic myths, modern technological myths, or even myths of contemporary theories. But if we do this we will, unwillingly, be the target of the text's very criticism.

We might, on the other hand, cultivate a "creative paranoia," making sense by creating our own individual pattern in order to understand the seeming contingency of the fictional world. Or we might, like other characters, try to reach beyond our linear and totalizing conceptions of history or texts and respond to Pynchon's alien voices, scattered all over the text's history of World War II, and of contemporary America.

Not by wrath does one kill but by laughter.
Come let us kill the spirit of gravity!
—FRIEDRICH NIETZSCHE

Chronology

1937   Thomas Pynchon born on May 8 in Glen Cove, Long Island.

1958   Graduates from Cornell University. Editorial writer at Boeing Company, Seattle.

1963   *V.* published. Pynchon receives Faulkner Prize for best first novel.

1966   *The Crying of Lot 49.*

1973   *Gravity's Rainbow.*

1984   *Slow Learner* (a collection of short stories).

Contributors

HAROLD BLOOM, Sterling Professor of the Humanities at Yale University, is the author of *The Anxiety of Influence, Poetry and Repression,* and many other volumes of literary criticism. His forthcoming study, *Freud: Transference and Authority,* attempts a full-scale reading of all of Freud's major writings. A MacArthur Prize Fellow, he is general editor of five series of literary criticism published by Chelsea House.

RICHARD POIRIER is one of the editors of *Raritan,* and of the Library of America. He is Professor of English at Rutgers University, and his books include studies of Mailer and Robert Frost, as well as *A World Elsewhere* and *The Performing Self.*

PAUL FUSSELL is Professor of English at the University of Pennsylvania. He is the author of studies of the eighteenth century and of *Poetic Meter and Poetic Form.* His study *The Great War and Modern Memory* won a National Book Award.

EDWARD MENDELSON is Professor of English at Columbia University. He is the author of several studies on W. H. Auden and is the literary executor of Auden's estate.

LOUIS MACKEY teaches in the Philosophy and Comparative Literature departments at the University of Texas at Austin. He has written studies on Kierkegaard, medieval philosophy, and philosophy of literature.

TONY TANNER is Reader in English at Cambridge University. His books include *The Reign of Wonder, City of Words,* and *Adultery in the Novel.*

CRAIG HANSEN WERNER teaches in the English Department at the University of Mississippi. He is the author of *Paradoxical Resolutions: American Fiction Since James Joyce.*

GABRIELE SCHWAB is Associate Professor of English at the University of Wisconsin, Milwaukee. She has written in German on Samuel Beckett and on modern fiction, and has published essays in English in *Yale French Studies* and *New Literary History.*

Bibliography

Bloom, Harold, ed. *Modern Critical Views: Thomas Pynchon.* New Haven, Conn.: Chelsea House, 1986.

Cowart, David. *Thomas Pynchon: The Art of Allusion.* Carbondale: Southern Illinois University Press, 1980.

Davis, Robert Murray. "Parody, Paranoia, and the Dead End of Language." *Genre* 5 (1972): 367–77.

Fowler, Douglas. "Pynchon's Magic World." *South Atlantic Quarterly* 79, no. 1 (1980): 51–60.

Hausdorff, Don. "Thomas Pynchon's Multiple Absurdities." *Wisconsin Studies in Contemporary Literature* 7 (1966): 158–69.

Henderson, Harry B., III. *Versions of the Past.* New York: Oxford University Press, 1974.

Kirby, David K. "Two Modern Versions of the Quest." *Southern Humanities Review* 5 (1971): 387–95.

Levine, George, and David Leverenz, eds. *Mindful Pleasures: Essays on Thomas Pynchon.* Boston: Little, Brown, 1976.

Lewis, R. W. B. *Trials of the Word.* New Haven: Yale University Press, 1965.

McConnell, Frank D. "Thomas Pynchon." In *Contemporary Novelists,* edited by James Vinson, 1033–36. London: St. James Press, 1972.

Marquez, Antonio C. "Everything is Connected: Paranoia in *Gravity's Rainbow.*" *Perspectives on Contemporary Literature* 9 (1983): 92–104.

Mendelson, Edward, ed. *Pynchon: A Collection of Critical Essays.* Englewood Cliffs, N. J.: Prentice-Hall, 1978.

Olderman, Raymond S. *Beyond the Waste Land: A Study of the American Novel in the Nineteen Sixties.* New Haven: Yale University Press, 1972.

Ozier, Lance W. "Antipointsman / Antimexico: Some Mathematical Imagery in *Gravity's Rainbow.*" *Critique* 16, no. 2 (1974): 73–90.

Pearce, Richard, ed. *Critical Essays on Thomas Pynchon.* Boston: G. K. Hall, 1981.

Plater, William. *The Grim Phoenix.* Bloomington: Indiana University Press, 1978.

Richter, David. *Fable's End.* Chicago: The University of Chicago Press, 1974.

Schmitz, Neil. "Describing the Demon: The Appeal of Thomas Pynchon." *Partisan Review* 42 (1975): 112–25.

Schwartz, Richard Alan. "Thomas Pynchon and the Evolution of Fiction." *Science Fiction Studies* 8, no. 2 (1981): 165–72.

Siegel, Mark. *Creative Paranoia in* Gravity's Rainbow. Port Washington, N.Y.: Kennikat Press, 1978.

Simmon, Scott. "A Character Index: *Gravity's Rainbow.*" *Critique* 16, no. 2 (1974): 68–72.

———. "*Gravity's Rainbow* Described." *Critique* 16, no. 2 (1974): 54–67.

Slade, Joseph. *Thomas Pynchon.* New York: Warner Paperbacks, 1974.

Solberg, Sara M. "On Comparing Apples and Oranges: James Joyce and Thomas Pynchon." *Comparative Literature Studies* 16, no. 1 (1979): 33–40.

Tanner, Tony. *City of Words.* New York: Harper and Row, 1971.

———. *Thomas Pynchon.* London: Methuen and Co., 1982.

Thiher, Alan. "Kafka's Legacy." *Modern Fiction Studies* 26 (1981): 543–62.

Trachtenberg, Stanley. "Counterhumor: Comedy in Contemporary American Fiction." *Georgia Review* 27, no. 1 (1973): 33–48.

Twentieth Century Literature 21, no. 2 (1975). Special Thomas Pynchon issue.

Vidal, Gore. "American Plastic: The Matter of Fiction." In *Matters of Fact and Fiction: Essays 1973–1976.* New York: Random House, 1977.

Wagner, Linda W. "A Note on Oedipa the Roadrunner." *Journal of Narrative Technique* 4 (1974): 155–61.

Weixlmann, Joseph. "Thomas Pynchon: A Bibliography." *Critique* 14, no. 2 (1972): 34–43.

Wood, Michael. "Joyce's Influenza." *The New York Review of Books* 13 October 1977.

Young, James Dean. "The Enigma Variations of Thomas Pynchon." *Critique* 10 (1968): 69–77.

Acknowledgments

"Rocket Power" by Richard Poirier from *Saturday Review of the Arts* 1, no. 3 (3 March 1973), © 1973 by *Saturday Review* Company. Reprinted by permission.

"The Ritual of Military Memory" (originally entitled "Persistence and Memory: The Ritual of Military Memory") by Paul Fussell from *The Great War and Modern Memory* by Paul Fussell, © 1975 by Oxford University Press, Inc. Reprinted by permission.

"Gravity's Encyclopedia" by Edward Mendelson from *Mindful Pleasures: Essays on Thomas Pynchon,* edited by George Levine and David Leverenz, © 1976 by George Levine and David Leverenz. Reprinted by permission of Little, Brown & Co.

"Paranoia, Pynchon, and Preterition" by Louis Mackey from *Sub-Stance,* no. 30 (Winter 1981), © 1981 by Sub-Stance, Inc. Reprinted by permission of the University of Wisconsin Press.

"*Gravity's Rainbow:* An Experience in Modern Reading" (originally entitled "*Gravity's Rainbow*") by Tony Tanner from *Thomas Pynchon* by Tony Tanner, © 1982 by Tony Tanner. Reprinted by permission.

"Recognizing Reality, Realizing Responsibility" (originally entitled "Recognizing Reality, Realizing Responsibility: Joyce, Gaddis, Pynchon") by Craig Hansen Werner from *Paradoxical Resolutions: American Fiction Since James Joyce* by Craig Hansen Werner, © 1982 by the Board of Trustees of the University of Illinois. Reprinted by permission of the University of Illinois Press and the author.

"Creative Paranoia and Frost Patterns of White Words" (originally entitled "Creative Paranoia and Frost Patterns of White Words: Making Sense in and of *Gravity's Rainbow*") by Gabriele Schwab from *Making Sense,* edited by Gerhard Hoffmann, © 1986 by Fink Verlag, Munich. Reprinted by permission of the editor and the author. This essay originally appeared in *Center for Twentieth Century Studies,* no. 4 (Fall 1985), The University of Wisconsin-Milwaukee.

Index